HOW TO PROTECT YOUR INCOME IN YOUR SENIOR YEARS

101 LETTERS TO ANSWER YOUR EVERY QUESTION

How to deal with the government.

Know the benefits you are entitled to and how to obtain them. Form letters are included. (Just copy them with your name and address.)

Know your rights as a Senior Citizen.

Learn how to survive in the 90's.

What you can do about age discrimination in employment.

Addresses for government agencies included.

written by **Harvey Kule** ISBN #1-879191-04-0 Copyright 1991 — The Forms Man, Inc.

TABLE OF CONTENTS

CHAPTERS:

I: What Your Government Owes You   3

II: Applying For Social Security   17

III: Knowing More About SSI   36

IV: What You Should Know About Private Pensions   47

V: IRAs And Other Investments   61

VI: Medicare, Medicaid And Nursing Homes   77

VII: Knowing More About Earned Income   89

VIII: Tax Credits And Disability   99

IX: Fighting Age Discrimination In Employment   110

X: Estate Planning   120

Appendixes:

I: Medicare Carriers By State   131
II: Monthly Benefits At Age 65   133
III: Checklist Of Essential Documents   134
IV: Aging Information State Directory   135
V: Social Security Administration (SSA)
      SSA Regional Office Telephone Contacts   137
      SSA Regional Office Addresses   138
      SSA Headquarters   139
VI: U.S. Labor Department, Labor-Management
      Services Administration (LMSA)   140
VII: National Organizations For The Elderly   141
VIII: List of Charts, Tables, and Forms   143
IX: List of Questions   144

I: WHAT YOUR GOVERNMENT OWES YOU

1. What Is Social Security?

DEAR MR. ANSWERMAN: I've been having an argument with a friend of mine at work. I say that the government owes us something when we're ready to retire. He keeps quoting from President Kennedy's speech, "Ask not what your government owes you, but what you owe your government." I would like your opinion on this subject.

Marilyn G., New Castle, KY

HOW TO EARN SOCIAL SECURITY CREDITS:

--Work on a job covered by Social Security
--You earn 1 credit for every quarter of coverage if you have a certain amount of earnings. The amount of covered earnings needed for credit automatically rises each year to keep up with increases in average wage levels.
--You can earn up to 4 credits each year, but no more, regardless of the amount of money earned.
--In 1990, you can earn 1 credit for each $520 of your covered annual earnings to a maximum of 4 credits for 1990.

DEAR MARILYN G: Kennedy's words were: "Ask not what your country can do for you: Ask what you can do for your country."

But if you have been working and paying Social Security taxes, then you have given what the federal government has asked for and you will be entitled to benefits when you retire.

The Social Security Act was passed in 1935. It provides income protection to workers and their families in the event of retirement, death, or disability.

This act is administered by the Social Security Administration (SSA). While the SSA administers a number of other programs besides old age retirement, the main program for you to consider for your retirement benefits is Social Security.

When you are working and paying Social Security taxes, you are earning credits which go towards your retirement benefits. If you look at your pay stubs, you should see a section marked FICA. The amount of your FICA deductions shows the Social Security taxes you are paying.

The number of credits you need to get retirement benefits depends on your date of birth. If you were born in 1929 or later, you need 40 credits, or about 10 years of work. Most people earn many more credits than they need to qualify for Social Security.

2. How Much Will My Retirement Benefit Be?

DEAR MR. ANSWERMAN: I've been a commissioned salesman for most of my working life. Some years were great and others weren't so good. I'm 60 years old now. Would the unevenness of my earnings affect my Social Security retirement benefits?

Joseph K., Los Angeles, CA

WHEN COMMISSIONS ARE WAGES:

--When a salesperson is an employee
--When commissions are the sole pay and no advances are given
--When advances are made against future commissions, they are counted in the year they were paid.

SPECIAL PROVISION WHEN SELF-EMPLOYMENT EARNINGS ARE LOW:

--When an individual has at least $400 per year in earnings in two of the preceding three years and his gross income from self-employment is $2400 or less, the person may report either the actual net income or two-thirds of gross income.
--Individuals and partnerships may report actual net income or $1600 when gross income is over $1600, but less than $2400.

DEAR JOSEPH K: Your benefit amount is based on your earnings averaged over most of your working career. Higher lifetime earnings result in higher benefits. If you have some years of no earnings or low earnings, your benefit amount may be lower than if you had a consistently high earning history.

Your benefit amount also is affected by your age at the time you start receiving benefits. If you start your retirement benefits at age 62, the earliest possible retirement age, your benefit will be lower than if you waited until a later age.

If you call the toll-free telephone number 1-800-772-1213, you can receive a Request for Earnings and Benefit Estimate Statement. When you mail in this form, which is shown in this book, Social Security will mail back your complete earnings history along with estimates of your benefits for retirement at age 62, full retirement age, or age 70. It will also give you estimates of disability or survivors benefits that might be payable.

Also check with the table on the next page which shows some approximate monthly benefits for workers with steady earnings. While you might not be in the category of a steady earning worker, you may get some idea of what range you are in.

The amount of benefits you receive will also automatically increase with rises in the cost-of living index.

Approximate Monthly Benefits If You Retire At Full Retirement Age And Had Steady Lifetime Earnings

Your Age In 1991	Your Family	Your Earnings In 1990				
		$20,000	$30,000	$40,000	$50,000	$51,300 Or More[1]
45	You	$ 863	$1,124	$1,263	$1,392	$1,422
	You and your spouse[2]	1,294	1,686	1,894	2,088	2,133
55	You	783	1,014	1,106	1,181	1,195
	You and your spouse[2]	1,174	1,521	1,659	1,771	1,792
65	You	725	926	982	1,021	1,022
	You and your spouse[2]	1,087	1,389	1,473	1,531	1,533

[1] Use this column if you earn more than the maximum Social Security earnings base.

[2] Your spouse is assumed to be the same age as you. Your spouse may qualify for a higher retirement benefit based on his or her own work record.

Note: The accuracy of these estimates depends on the pattern of your actual past earnings, and on your earnings in the future.

Write to the address below for a copy of the Request for Earnings and Benefit Estimate Statement form. A copy of this form is duplicated on the next page.

SOCIAL SECURITY ADMINISTRATION
SALINAS DATA OPERATIONS CENTER
100 E. ALVIN DRIVE
SALINAS, CA 93906-2494

SOCIAL SECURITY ADMINISTRATION

Request for Earnings and Benefit Estimate Statement

To receive a free statement of your earnings covered by Social Security and your estimated future benefits, all you need to do is fill out this form. Please print or type your answers. When you have completed the form, fold it and mail it to us.

1. Name shown on your Social Security card:

First _____ Middle Initial _____ Last _____

2. Your Social Security number as shown on your card:

☐☐☐ - ☐☐ - ☐☐☐☐

3. Your date of birth: Month _____ Day _____ Year _____

4. Other Social Security numbers you have used:

☐☐☐ - ☐☐ - ☐☐☐☐
☐☐☐ - ☐☐ - ☐☐☐☐

5. Your Sex: ☐ Male ☐ Female

6. Other names you have used (including a maiden name):

_____

7. Show your actual earnings for last year and your estimated earnings for this year. Include only wages and/or net self-employment income covered by Social Security.

A. Last year's actual earnings:

$ ☐☐☐ , ☐☐☐ . 0 0
Dollars only

B. This year's estimated earnings:

$ ☐☐☐ , ☐☐☐ . 0 0
Dollars only

8. Show the age at which you plan to retire: ☐☐
(Show only one age)

9. Below, show the average yearly amount that you think you will earn between now and when you plan to retire. Your estimate of future earnings will be added to those earnings already on our records to give you the best possible estimate.

Enter a yearly average, not your total future lifetime earnings. Only show earnings covered by Social Security. Do not add cost-of-living, performance or scheduled pay increases or bonuses. The reason for this is that we estimate retirement benefits in today's dollars, but adjust them to account for average wage growth in the national economy.

However, if you expect to earn significantly more or less in the future due to promotions, job changes, part-time work, or an absence from the work force, enter the amount in today's dollars that most closely reflects your future average yearly earnings.

Most people should enter the same amount that they are earning now (the amount shown in 7B).

Your future average yearly earnings:

$ ☐☐☐ , ☐☐☐ . 0 0
Dollars only

10. Address where you want us to send the statement:

Name _____

Street Address (Include Apt. No., P.O. Box, or Rural Route) _____

City _____ State _____ Zip Code _____

I am asking for information about my own Social Security record or the record of a person I am authorized to represent. I understand that if I deliberately request information under false pretenses I may be guilty of a federal crime and could be fined and/or imprisoned. I authorize you to send the statement of earnings and benefit estimates to the person named in item 10 through a contractor.

Please sign your name (Do not print)

Date _____ (Area Code) Daytime Telephone No. _____

ABOUT THE PRIVACY ACT

Social Security is allowed to collect the facts on this form under Section 205 of the Social Security Act. We need them to quickly identify your record and prepare the earnings statement you asked us for. Giving us these facts is voluntary. However, without them we may not be able to give you an earnings and benefit estimate statement. Neither the Social Security Administration nor its contractor will use the information for any other purpose.

6

Form SSA-7004-PC-OP2 (9-89) Destroy prior editions

3. What Is Full Retirement Age?

DEAR MR. ANSWERMAN: I'm a little confused about the exact age I can begin to collect Social Security benefits. Some people say I can begin when I reach age 62 and others say at age 65. Now I'm also hearing that the new age is 67. Can you clarify this problem for me?

Norman S., Waterloo, IA

TESTS TO DETERMINE IF A PERSON HAS BECOME FULLY INSURED:

--A person has 40 quarters of coverage, which is a total of 10 years of covered work
--A person has at least six quarters of coverage and died prior to 1951
--A person has at least one quarter of coverage acquired after 1936 for each calendar year after 1950 or after reaching age 21 and before reaching age 62 or dies or becomes disabled

--Do not count any year in which there was a period of disability.
--From October 1960 through July 1961 fully insured status was based on 1 quarter of coverage for every 3 elapsed quarters.
--Before October 1960 a 1 for 2 provision was applied.

DEAR NORMAN S: All three answers are correct, but it needs to be explained. The usual retirement age for people retiring now is age 65. Social Security calls this "full retirement age," and the benefit amount that is payable is considered the full retirement benefit.

Because of longer life expectancies, the full retirement age will be increased in gradual steps until it reaches age 67. This change starts in the year 2000, and it affects people born in 1938 and later.

If you check with the chart on the next page, you'll get a better idea of how your birthday affects your waiting time for full benefits.

As for the age 62, you can start your Social Security benefits as early as age 62, but the benefit amount you receive will be less than your full retirement benefit.

The reduction for starting your Social Security at age 62 is 20 percent; at age 63, it is 13 1/3 percent; and at age 64, it is 6 2/3 percent.

If your full retirement age is older than 65 because you were born after 1937, you still will be able to take your retirement benefits at age 62, but the reduction in your benefit amount will be greater than it is for people retiring now.

As a general rule, early retirement will give you about the same total Social Security benefits over your lifetime, but in smaller amounts, to take into account the longer period you will receive them.

Age To Receive Full Social Security Benefits

Year Of Birth	Full Retirement Age
1937 or earlier	65
1938	65 and 2 months
1939	65 and 4 months
1940	65 and 6 months
1941	65 and 8 months
1942	65 and 10 months
1943—1954	66
1955	66 and 2 months
1956	66 and 4 months
1957	66 and 6 months
1958	66 and 8 months
1959	66 and 10 months
1960 and later	67

Chart Of Increases For Delayed Retirement

Year Of Birth	Yearly Percentage Increase
1916 or earlier	1%
1917 — 1924	3%
1925 — 1926	3.5%
1927 — 1928	4%
1929 — 1930	4.5%
1931 — 1932	5%
1933 — 1934	5.5%
1935 — 1936	6%
1937 — 1938	6.5%
1939 — 1940	7%
1941 — 1942	7.5%
1943 or later	8%

4. What Is Delayed Retirement?

DEAR MR. ANSWERMAN: My wife and I are running a comfortable business from our home. We are not hassled by bosses and the age factor does not seem to slow us up in the kind of work we do, which is a professional service. We therefore do not feel the rush to retire at age 65, if we do not have to.

Could you tell me if there are any advantages in delaying our retirement?

Sylvia H., Lowell, MA

DELAYED RETIREMENT CREDIT RATES:

Year Attain Age 62	Annual Percent
1979-1986	3%
1987-1988	3.5%
1989-1990	4%
1991-1992	4.5%
1993-1994	5%
1995-1996	5.5%
1997-1998	6%
1999-2000	6.5%
2001-2002	7%
2003-2004	7.5%
2005 or after	8%

DEAR SYLVIA H: If you decide to continue working full time beyond your full retirement age, you can increase your Social Security benefit in two ways:

1. If you're like most people who delay their retirement, you'll be adding a year of high earnings to your Social Security record. Higher lifetime earnings result in higher benefits.

2. In addition, your benefit will be increased by a certain percentage if you delay retirement. These increases will be added in automatically from the time you reach your full retirement age until you start taking your benefits, or you reach age 70. The percentage varies depending on your date of birth.

From the chart you can see that if you were born in 1943 or later, Social Security will add an extra 8 percent to your benefit for each year you delay signing up for Social Security beyond your full retirement age.

But there is an important point to keep in mind. If you delay your retirement, be sure to sign up for Medicare at age 65. Under certain conditions, medical insurance costs more if you delay applying for it.

5. Is Social Security Enough By Itself?

DEAR MR. ANSWERMAN: I just sent off for a Benefit Estimate Statement from Social Security. Given what you know about minimum and maximum benefits that a person could receive from Social Security, what are the chances that Social Security alone is all you need to finance your retirement?

Delores M., Gadsden, AL

CHECKLIST OF SOURCES FOR POTENTIAL RETIREMENT INCOME TO SUPPLEMENT SOCIAL SECURITY:

--Other government pensions from Civil Service, Veterans, and Railroad Retirement funds
--Private company pension funds
--Employment salary or wages
--Cash accounts: checking, passbook savings, CDs, money market funds
--Life insurance annuities
--IRA and Keogh plans
--Stock and bond dividends
--Corporate and government securities
--Mutual funds
--Real estate
--Collectibles
--Sale of home or business

DEAR DELORES M: A worker who turned 65 in 1991 and who always earned the maximum amount covered by Social Security will receive a benefit of $1022 and a couple will receive $1,533. Even if a spouse has never earned an income, the spouse is entitled to receive benefits.

On the low side, a couple could receive $753 with a present annual earnings of $12,000.

Given the high cost of living in most places today, the majority of retirees would find these maximum and minimum figures inadequate for a comfortable lifestyle, although there might be some who would not have too much difficulty adjusting to the figure if they had to.

Social Security was and is designed to provide a base for retirement income. The rest should come from pensions, savings and investment.

If you retire with the maximum Social Security benefit you will be receiving about 27 percent of your preretirement pay. If you retire with the U.S. average of lifetime earnings, you will be receiving about 41 percent of your lifetime pay.

Review the checklist on the left for other retirement income sources.

Percent of the aged receiving social security benefits

Age	Percent
55-61	13
62-64	49
65 and over	89
70-72	90
73 and over	90

6. What If I Work After Retirement?

DEAR ANSWERMAN: I would like to continue working after I retire, but I haven't decided whether it should be part-time or full-time employment. I would also like to collect as much of my Social Security benefit as possible. Could you advise me as to how much work I can do to collect the maximum amount of my Social Security when I retire?

Arnold L., Clearwater, FL

EMPLOYMENT OF RETIRED PERSONS:

--Approximately 12 percent of persons over the age of 65 were working or looking for work in 1989, representing about 3.4 million people.
--Of these, 17 percent or 2 million were men and 8 percent or 1.4 million were women.
--Approximately 2.6 percent were unemployed.
--Approximately half of those working over the age of 65 were working part time.
--About 25 percent of those working over the age of 65 were self-employed. In numbers this was about 825,000.

DEAR ARNOLD L: You can continue to work and still get retirement benefits as long as your earnings are under certain limits.

These limits increase each year as average wages increase. In 1991, the earnings limits were $7,080 for people under 65 and $9,720 for people age 65 to 69. People who are 70 or older do not have an earnings limit.

You can work and earn up to the limit and still get all your Social Security checks. If your earnings go over the limit, some or all of your benefits will be offset by your earnings.

In 1991, $1.00 in benefits was withheld for every $3.00 in earnings above the limit for people aged 65 to 69. For persons under 65, $1.00 was withheld for every $2.00 in earnings above the limit. Only earned income counts. Income from savings, investments, pensions, or insurance does not count in calculating the earnings test.

Ask your Social Security office for the pamphlet, "If You Work After You Retire," and a factsheet titled, "How Work Affects Your Social Security Benefits." These will give you all the details on this subject and can help you decide how working will affect your benefits.

There are other things to consider when thinking about working after retirement. They include the state of your health, your leisure time interests, hobbies, family, and your personal preferences. Some people love retirement, while others love to work.

7. What Portion Of My Social Security Will Be Taxed?

DEAR MR. ANSWERMAN: My gross income for last year was over $25,000. As a widower, I am collecting my wife's Social Security benefits. How much of the Social Security benefit will be taxable?

Roy C., Goshen, AR

AVOIDING FEDERAL ESTATE TAXES:

--Deaths after 1987, no tax on amounts up to $600,000
--Review the 1976 Tax Reform Act
--Review the 1981 Economic Recovery Tax Act
--Transfer parts of your estate to your spouse tax-free
--Make gifts of up to $10,000 per year tax-free to as many recipients as you wish (annual exclusion)
--Make contributions to charity

DEAR ROY C: Most people do not pay income taxes on their Social Security benefits. However, beneficiaries whose adjusted gross income, plus one half of their Social Security beneftis, exceeds certain thresholds can have up to one half of their benefits subject to the Federal income tax.

The thresholds are $25,000 for a single individual and $32,000 for couples.

Look for the worksheet in the booklet that comes with your 1040 income tax form. This explains how to compute the amount of your benefits that may be taxable.

Some states currently include Social Security benefits in income subject to their state income tax.

You can call the Internal Revenue Service toll free by dialing 1-800-829-3676. Ask for Publication 554, "Tax Benefits for Older Americans," and Publication 915, "Tax Information on Social Security."

A copy of the worksheet for computing your tax in this situation is reproduced on the next page.

Of course, if you are making over the limit, it is a good idea to review your situation with a professional tax advisor. The tax laws today are very complex and most of us need some help to be sure that we are getting all the deductions we are eligible to receive.

Social Security and Equivalent Railroad Retirement Benefits
Worksheet #1
(Keep for your records)

Check only one box:

☐ **A.** Single—enter $25,000 on line 8 below.

☐ **B.** Married filing a joint return—enter $32,000 on line 8 below.

☐ **C.** Married not filing a joint return and lived with your spouse at any time during the year—enter –0– on line 8 below.

☐ **D.** Married not filing a joint return and DID NOT live with your spouse at any time during the year—enter $25,000 on line 8 below.

1. Enter the total amount from Box 5 of ALL your Forms SSA–1099 and Forms RRB–1099 (if applicable) .... **1.** _____

   Note. If line 1 is zero or less, stop here; none of your benefits are taxable. Otherwise, go on to line 2.

2. Divide the amount on line 1 by 2 .... **2.** _____

3. Add the amounts on your 1990 Form 1040, lines 7, 8a, 8b through 20, plus line 22. Do not include here any amounts from lines 16a or 17a of Form 1040, or from Box 5 of Forms SSA–1099 or RRB–1099 .... **3.** _____

4. Enter the amount of any U.S. savings bond interest exclusion, foreign earned income exclusion, foreign housing exclusion, exclusion of income from U.S. possessions, or exclusion of income from Puerto Rico by bona fide residents of Puerto Rico that you claimed .... **4.** _____

5. Add lines 2, 3, and 4 .... **5.** _____

6. Enter the amount from Form 1040, lines 24 through 29, plus any write-in amounts on line 30 (other than the foreign housing deduction) .... **6.** _____

7. Subtract line 6 from line 5.. **7.** _____

8. Enter:

   $25,000 if you checked Box **A** or **D,** or

   $32,000 if you checked Box **B,** or

   –0– if you checked Box **C**... **8.** _____

9. Subtract line 8 from line 7... **9.** _____

   Note: If line 9 is zero, stop here. None of your benefits are taxable. Do not enter any amounts on Form 1040, lines 21a or 21b, unless you checked Box D above. If you checked Box D, enter –0– on line 21b and write "D" to the left of line 21a. If line 9 is more than zero, go on to line 10.

10. Divide the amount on line 9 by 2 .... **10.** _____

11. **Taxable benefits.**

    • First, enter on Form 1040, line 21a, the amount from line 1 above.

    • Then, compare the amounts on lines 2 and 10 above, and enter the **smaller** of the two amounts on this line. Also enter this amount on Form 1040, line 21b (unless you make the lump-sum election for benefits attributable to earlier year(s)).............................. **11.** _____

Note: Use this worksheet whether or not you received a lump-sum payment. If you received a lump-sum payment in this year that was for an earlier year, see *Lump-Sum Benefits,* earlier. As that discussion suggests (under *Making the election*), complete Worksheets #2 and #3 to see whether you can report a lower taxable benefit.

13

8. How Do I Appeal A Decision On My Social Security Benefit?

DEAR MR. ANSWERMAN: I recently applied to Social Security to find out why my benefits are less than my records show they should be. I feel Social Security did not calculate all my earnings over the years. How do I go about appealing the decision that Social Security made about my benefits?

If it is decided that they made a mistake and I am entitled to a larger monthly benefit, will Social Security pay me a lump sum for the period they underpaid me?

Diana B., Waterbury, CT

FACTS ABOUT APPEALS:

--Use Form HA-501
--Requests must be made within 60 days
--There is not cost
--You may represent yourself
--You may choose someone to represent you
--The amount being appealed must be more than $100
--Hearings are held with 75 miles of a person's home
--Notice must be at least 10 days in advance of a hearing
--Notices of reconsideration must include the Social Security number of the claimant, the reason for disagreement, additional evidence to be submitted, and the name and address of any representative

DEAR DIANA B: Social Security does have an appeal process when there is a disagreement between a claimant and the Social Security Administration. These are the steps to follow:

FIRST: You must request that the initial determination be reconsidered. A reconsideration is a reexamination of the adminstrative records.

SECOND: If there is still a disagreement after the reconsideration, you may request a hearing before an administrative law judge.

THIRD: The next step, if there is still a disagreement after a hearing, is a review of the decision by the Appeals Council of the Office of Hearings and Appeals. They may deny or grant a review.

FOURTH: If an appeal is denied, the claimant may file a civil action in U.S. District Court.

FIFTH: There are time limitations in this process that a claimant must be aware of. You may want a representative to help you with this process. This will be discussed in my answer to the next question.

If the judgment is in your favor, you will get a lump sum payment.

9. Am I Allowed To Have A Representative Help Me With My Claim?

DEAR MR. ANSWERMAN: Recently I got involved with Social Security over a claim. The accountant I used in my business tells me that he has a lot of experience dealing with the kind of claim I am making with Social Security. Will I have any problem appointing him as my representative? Or would I be better off using an attorney?

William W., Macon, GA

WHAT YOUR REPRESENTATIVE CAN DO FOR YOU:

--Get information from your file
--Submit evidence to support your claim
--Come to a Social Security interview with you
--Request reconsideration, hearing, or appeal
--Give you moral support, as well as professional guidance in making your claim and seeing you through the appeals process

DEAR WILLIAM W: You may appoint any individual to be your representative, but not a corporation, firm, or organization to represent you, nor someone who has been suspended or prohibited by Social Security from representing individuals.

You must appoint your representative in writing. Use the form SSa-1696-U3, "Appointment of Representative" or a plain piece of paper for this purpose. State the name of the person you are appointing and sign your name. If the person is not an attorney, he or she must state in writing his or her name, the acceptance of the appointment as your representative, and sign the form or paper.

Your representative can charge the amount that Social Security determines. It will hold back only 25 percent of any past due payments and the approved fee will be paid from this money to the attorney. You will receive the remainder.

Be sure that your attorney, if you use one as your representative, is qualified to be your representative for Social Security proceedings.

Be sure that your attorney or representative knows that the fees charged are restricted by the Social Security Administration. Discuss these matters prior to engaging the services of anyone to represent you. And get an agreement between you in writing.

10. How Much Can My Spouse And Children Get?

DEAR MR. ANSWERMAN: Both my husband and I are eligible for Social Security benefits. I am concerned about family benefits because we also have two children that we have to take care of. Will I only get half of his benefit or I am entitled to my own benefit? I have worked full time throughout our marriage. Will the children be entitled to any benefits?

Ellen O., Topeka, KS

SOME BENEFIT FIGURES:

Average Monthly Earnings	*Total Worker and Spouse*
$4275	$1818
3550	1654
3100	1554
2900	1509
2550	1429
2100	1317
1900	1221
1800	1173
1600	1077
1400	981
1200	885
1000	789
800	675

DEAR ELLEN O: The full benefit for a spouse is one half of the retired worker's full benefit. If your spouse takes benefits before the age of 65, the amount is reduced. At 62 it can be as low as 37.5 percent. A spouse who is taking care of a child who is under 16 or disabled gets full benefits, regardless of age. The full benefit for a spouse is 50 percent of the spouse's benefit.

If you are eligible for both your own retirement benefits and for benefits as a spouse, you will get the higher amount.

There is a limit to the amount of money that can be paid to a family. If the total benefits due your spouse and children exceed the limit, their benefits will be reduced proportionately, but your benefit will not be affected.

Here is a list of family member benefits:

* Wife or husband aged 62 or older
* Wife or husband under 62, who is taking care of a child under 16 or disabled
* Former wife or husband age 62 or older
* Children up to age 18
* Children aged 18-19 if they attend high school or grade school
* Children over 18 who are disabled

II: APPLYING FOR SOCIAL SECURITY

1. What Will I Need To Apply For Social Security?

DEAR MR. ANSWERMAN: I'll be turning 65 in four months and I would like to know if it is too early to apply for Social Security. Also, what will I need to show them at Social Security?

Sarah D., Portland, ME

HINTS WHEN APPLYING FOR SOCIAL SECURITY BENEFITS:

--Applications are considered to be filed as of the day it is received by the Social Security office
--A U.S. postmark on the envelope may be used as the applicable date
--The proper application forms must be used
--The form must be complete
--All items must be filled in. If you don't know the answer to a question, write "unknown."
--File your claim with the correct office
--Statements for claims must be made clearly
--Use the Social Security office for help free of charge in filling out applications
--In cases when the claimant is in poor health, arrangements can be made to have someone from Social Security come to the person's home

DEAR ELLEN O: You can apply up to 3 months before the date you want your benefits to start. You can apply for benefits by telephone or by going to any social security office.

Even though there are a number of documents you will need, it is a good idea not to delay your application because you do not have all the information. Social Security can help you get the ones you may not have.

Here is a list of some of the things you will need:

--Your Social Security number
--Your birth certificate
--Your W-2 forms or self-employment tax return for last year
--Your spouse's birth certificate and Social Security number if he or she is applying for benefits
--Children's birth certificates and Social Security numbers, if applying for children's benefits
--Your checking or savings account information if you want direct deposit

You will need to submit original documents or copies certified by the issuing office. Social Security will make photcopies of these and return your documents. You can either bring these documents in with you to the Social Security office or you can mail them in.

2. How Can I Get Information About Social Security?

DEAR MR. ANSWERMAN: I have been trying to get information about Social Security, mainly some kind of manual that would give me basic information about the services of Social Security.

I dialed two numbers and the operator gave me a new number, which I then dialed. All I got when I dialed the new number was a busy signal.

On a flyer put out by Social Security that I picked up it said that the Social Security Adminstration is the best source of information. When I went down to my local office, I was told that the only information was on a rack by the wall. Most of the racks, unfortunately, were empty and I was only able to pick up one pamphlet and a couple of factsheets.

How can I get complete information about Social Security?

Randy N., Duluth, MN

FYI (FOR YOUR INFORMATION):

--*Social Security will make presentations before civic, labor, medical, farm, management, school, and other groups and organizations interest in the programs that it administers*
--*Pamphlets, manuals and factsheets are available from Social Security facilities*
--*Libraries carry publications of Social Security*
--*Informational Facilities at Social Security offices make copying available to the public*

DEAR RANDY N: Social Security recommends that since most calls occur during the first week of the month, and on Mondays and Tuesdays of other weeks, that you should call during other times of the month. In other words, make your calls after the first week of the month and call on Wednesdays, Thursdays, and Fridays.

If your business is urgent, however, then call early in the morning or late in the afternoon.

Social Security advises that you should not pay for information or service. Some businesses advertise that they can provide name changes, Social Security cards, or earning statements. These businesses charge a fee for these services. All of these services are provided to you free by Social Security.

There are a number of excellent manuals and books, nonetheless, that give detailed information that goes beyond the Social Security pamphlets and get into the laws that govern Social Security. Three that I like to recommend are:

--*The Rights of Older Persons,* ACLU, 1989.
--*Social Security Handbook,* Ninth Edition, 1986.
--*Social Security Manual,* National Underwriter Company, 1990

3. How Will My Pension From Non-Covered Work Affect My Social Security Benefits?

DEAR MR. ANSWERMAN: It just so happens that I will be receiving a pension from my current job when I reach the age of 62. I understand that I will also be eligible for Social Security credits at that age, which is when I plan to retire. Will my Social Security benefits be affected by my pension? And if it is, how will it be affected?

Virginia A., Phoenix, AZ

WHO IS EXEMPT FROM PENSION OFFSET:

--Anyone whose pension is based on work covered by Social Security on the last day of employment

--Anyone whose pension is not based on his or her earnings

--Anyone who received or who was eligible to receive the government pension before December 1982 and meets all the requirements for Social Security spouse benefits in effect in January 1977

--Anyone who received or was eligible to receive the Federal, State, or local government pension before July 1, 1983 and was receiving one-half support from her or his spouse

--Federal employees who switched to FERS on or before December 31, 1987

DEAR VIRGINIA A: If you receive a pension from a job that is not covered by Social Security, and you also have enough Social Security credits to be eligible for retirement or disability benefits, a different formula may be used to figure your Social Security benefit.

While your pension from your job that is not covered by Social Security is not affected by this different formula, the formula will result in a lower Social Security benefit for you.

The different formula is called the modified formula. It soes not affect survivor benefits. It only affects workers who reach age 62 or become disabled after 1985 and first become eligible after 1985 for a monthly pension that is based wholly or partly on work that is not covered by Social Security. With pensions, you are eligible to receive it if you meet the requirements of the pension, even if you continue to work.

The modified formula is used to calculate your Social Security benefit beginning with the first month for which you receive both a Social Security benefit and a pension from work that is not covered under Social Security.

19

CONDITIONS UNDER WHICH THE MODIFIED FORMULA DOES NOT APPLY:

--Federal workers hired after December 31, 1983
--Employees of nonprofit organizations after January 1, 1984 when they were mandatorily covered by Social Security
--Persons who have 30 or more years of substantial earnings under Social Security
--Pensioners whose pensions are based solely on railroad retirement employment
--Workers whose only work not under Social Security was before 1957

Reduced benefits for workers receiving benefits was phased in gradually for those who reached 62 or became disabled from 1986 through 1989. These are the phase-in factors as they apply to those receiving non-Social Security pensions:

YEAR	EARNINGS	YEAR	EARNINGS
1937-50	$ 900[1]	1979	$4,725
1951-54	900	1980	5,100
1955-58	1,050	1981	5,550
1959-65	1,200	1982	6,075
1966-67	1,650	1983	6,675
1968-71	1,950	1984	7,050
1972	2,250	1985	7,425
1973	2,700	1986	7,875
1974	3,300	1987	8,175
1975	3,525	1988	8,400
1976	3,825	1989	8,925
1977	4,125	1990	9,525
1978	4,425		

[1] Total credited earnings from 1937-50 are divided by $900 to get the number of years of coverage (maximum of 14 years).

Workers with 30 or more years of substantial Social Security coverage are not affected by the modified benefit formula. Workers with 21-29 years of such earnings will have the first factor reduced according to the following schedule:

YEARS OF COVERAGE	FIRST FACTOR
30 or more	90 percent
29	85 percent
28	80 percent
27	75 percent
26	70 percent
25	65 percent
24	60 percent
23	55 percent
22	50 percent
21	45 percent
20 or less	40 percent

You are credited with a year of coverage if your earnings equal or exceed the figures shown for each year in the chart below:

YEAR YOU BECAME 62 OR DISABLED	FIRST FACTOR
1986	80 percent
1987	70 percent
1988	60 percent
1989	50 percent
1990 or later	40 percent

A GUARANTEE IS PROVIDED TO PROTECT WORKERS WITH RELATIVELY LOW PENSIONS. THE REDUCTION CANNOT BE MORE THAN ONE-HALF OF THE PART OF THE PENSION BASED ON EARNINGS AFTER 1956 THAT WERE NOT COVERED BY SOCIAL SECURITY.

4. What Is Acceptable Proof Of Marriage?

DEAR MR. ANSWERMAN: I have been living with my present husband for twenty-five years, but we were never legally married. Does Social Security recognize common-law marriages? If they do not, how will this affect my Social Security benefits when I retire?

Shirley N., McCall, ID

DEAR SHIRLEY N: Some states recognize common-law marriages. A common-law marriage is accepted by Social Security as a valid one if the state in which the agreement was made recognizes such marriages.

If Social Security requires proof of a common-law marriage, it can be established in a number of ways. Each parnter should submit an affidavit confirming the agreement to live together as husband and wife. And each one should get a statement from a blood relative confirming the agreement.

Can More Than One Spouse Receive Benefits From A Marriage?

DEAR MR. ANSWERMAN: I am married to a man who was married two times before he married me? Will this affect my Social Security benefits? Will his other wives be entitled to some of his benefits? If so, how much will they get and how much will I get?

Elizabeth R., Topeka, KS

DEAR ELIZABETH R: In most cases Social Security only pays a wife's or husband's benefits to one person. If a man has been married three times, only his current wife will receive benefits.

There is an exception to this, however. If a couple was married for at least 10 years before getting a divorce, Social Security will pay benefits to both the current spouse and the divorced one.

Sometimes it becomes necessary to establish that former marriages have been ended legally. A certified copy of a divorce decree will be necessary to prove that a marriage was legally ended.

In cases where a former spouse is already receiving benefits, the current spouse will be denied the right to any benefits.

5. What Is Acceptable Proof Of Age?

DEAR MR. ANSWERMAN: I am a naturalized American citizen. My family came to America from Hungary in 1931 when I was five years old. Whatever records we had seemed to have mysteriously disappeared. How will I prove my age when I apply for Social Security?

Jack E., Great Falls, MT

PROOF OF AGE DOCUMENTS--

--Birth certificate
--Baptismal record
--Immigration papers
--School records
--Census records
--Hospital records
--Insurance policies
--Marriage licenses
--Employment records
--Labor union records
--Military records
--Voting records
--Physician records
--Passports
--Family records
--Bible records

DEAR JACK E: For a person like yourself, who was born in a foreign country, the best proof of age comes from a record of entry into the United States, which will contain your declared age at that time. Your naturalization papers will also serve as a proof of age.

Other sources to prove age are public or church records of birth or baptism. Certified copies of these records can also be used as proof of age.

School or census records, insurance policies, marriage records, employment or labor union records, military records, voting records, passports, and physician's records of births are all sources to be used to prove age for the purposes of Social Security.

Often people who were born in another country have conflicting evidence of age. Some documents show one age and others show a different age. The Social Security Administration gives more weight to older documents than to recent ones.

If a dispute arises you can appeal your case. The court has been known to reverse decisions of the Administration regarding proof of age. In one case the court reversed a decision when the claimant submitted a corrected birth certificate. If you have evidence that may lead to a dispute, you should correct them as soon as possible and preferably before you reach the age when you feel you qualify for benefits.

6. How Do I Prove A Parent-Child Relationship?

DEAR MR. ANSWERMAN: About fifteen years ago I had a child by a woman who I was not married to. I have had custody and supported my son for all these years. I am about to retire and I believe that I will be able to claim benefits for him since he is not yet eighteen years old. Will I have any problem because I was not married to his mother?

David F., Joliet, IL

WHAT SOCIAL SECURITY RECOGNIZES AS AN INSURED WORKER'S CHILD:

--Legitmate child
--Any child who has the right under applicable State law to inherit personal property of the insured worker
--Stepchild
--Legally adopted child
--Child of a ceremonial marriage
--Natural child who has been acknowledged by the insured worker in writing
--Natural child if the insured worker has been ordered by the court to support the child
--Natural child when the court has decreed during the insured worker's lifetime to be the father
--Biological child
--Dependent grandchild

DEAR DAVID F: The evidence that you need to present is that the child has been living with you and that you have supported him throughout his life. You are eligible to claim benefits for him as a dependent child until he is eighteen.

Children of a retired, disabled, or deceased worker may also be eligible for Social Security benefits. The child may have to establish through official records that he or she is the child of the worker in question.

Income tax returns listing a child, a will referring to a child, an application for insurance that names the child, or a simple letter that acknowledges the child as his or her own are some acceptable ways to prove a parent-child relationship.

Hospital, church and school records may also be used, as well as statements from physicians, relatives or other people who acknowledge the relationship.

Illegitimate children can establish their eligibility if they can demonstrate that he or she can inherit the worker's personal property.

Adopted children can use court documents that dealt with the adoption procedure. Stepchildren need to establish that the child's natural parent is validly married to the insured worker.

For grandchildren to receive benefits, it is necessary to show that the grandchild was living with and received support from the grandparent. The child's parents in this type of case are either dead or disabled.

7. How Will I Be Notified By Social Security?

DEAR MR. ANSWERMAN: I recently applied for Social Security and have been waiting to hear from them. In the past when I dealt with the government, I often received phone calls for more information. Will Social Security notify me by mail or phone? If there is any problem with my application will they call me in for a meeting or will they just turn me down and will I have to start my application all over again?

George K., Reno, NV

FYI (FOR YOUR INFORMATION):

A number of lawsuits have been filed against the Social Security Administration when the agency has refused to provide a hearing before benefits were reduced or terminated.

The suits are based on the Fifth Amendment of the U.S. Constitution. It states that "no person shall be ... deprived of life, liberty or property, without due process of law."

DEAR GEORGE K: Most contacts from Social Security are made through the mail. You should receive your notice in the mail. If the decision is in your favor, the letter will specify the amount of your benefit.

When the decision is not favorable, the notice sent by Social Security is not likely to reveal the reason for the decision since they commonly use form letters when denying an application. These letters are vague and do not attempt to specifically tell you the reason for the denial.

The notification of denial will tell the receiver that the decision can be appealed and give an explanation about the appeal process.

If you are already receiving Social Security benefits and they are reduced or terminated, you are entitled to receive written notice of this decision and an explanation of your rights to appeal.

It is more usual to receive this type of notice before your benefits are reduced or terminated. You may lose your benefits or part of it while the appeal process is taking place.

In cases where the claimant wins the appeal, the claimant will receive retroactive benefits.

It is important when you are contacting Social Security to do so in writing and to keep all copies of the correspondence between you and the agency. You can only continue the appeal process when you have written documentation between you and the Social Security Administration about your claim to benefits.

8. Do I Have A Right To See My Social Security File?

DEAR MR. ANSWERMAN: I had some difficulty with an employer several years ago. When I went down to collect Unemployment Insurance there was no record of my having worked for the two years that I worked for this employer.

I'm concerned now that when I apply for Social Security my records will be incomplete because this employer failed to report my earnings. I'm also concerned about my Social Security record because I once applied for disability and there was a disagreement about the disposition of my medical problem.

How much if any of my Social Security file can I review?

Ceil K., Wilmington, DE

THE FOLLOWING FORMS ARE REPRODUCED AT THE END OF THIS CHAPTER:

--Report of Marriage/Divorce form
--Request for Benefit Recomputation form
--Request for Verification of Benefits form
--Start/Stop Work Notice for Social Security Retirement/Survivors Benefits form
--Change of Address for Social Security Checks form
--Report of Death form
--Document chart

DEAR CEIL K: You are entitled to see all of your Social Security file, except the medical information in it.

You can also have an authorized representative see this information. If you want others to see it, you may also authorize the information to be released to them.

You may have the medical information disclosed to you as well, but Social Security may decide to send it to your designated representative if they feel it may have an "adverse effect" on you.

Should Social Security refuse to disclose information from your file to you, you may sue them to obtain the information. You are guaranteed this right under the Freedom of Information Act. This act authorizes suits when federal agencies refuse to allow access to information about an individual by that person. Federal agencies must give people access to information they have on them.

You also have the right to have the information in your Social Security file kept secret. It is illegal for the Social Security Administration to disclose information from a file to any unauthorized person.

The only exceptions to this are that government agencies may give other government agencies certain information for authorized purposes.

Your Social Security number and some information about your coverage can sometimes be given to past and present employers. But on the whole, you are protected and can keep this information private.

9. Can A Creditor Attach My Social Security Benefits?

DEAR MR. ANSWERMAN: Last month I decided to buy a television on time. Due to the fact that I was short on cash, I fell behind in my payments. The store manager told me that he can attach my Social Security check to get his payments because I am paying for the set out of my Social Security check.

My friend tells me that the store manager is only trying to scare me and that he can't do that. Could you please advise me on this problem?

Peg W., Saginaw, MI

WHO CANNOT ATTACH YOUR SOCIAL SECURITY CHECK:

--Stores
--Loan companies
--State government
--Local government

WHO CAN ATTACH YOUR SOCIAL SECURITY CHECK:

--IRS
--Court ordered child support

DEAR PEG W: Don't let the store manager harass you. He cannot attach your Social Security check. The Social Security Act is very specific on this issue. It cannot be attached or garnished by a creditor.

If you owe money to a store or a loan company, your Social Security benefits cannot be attached by your creditor to collect your debts.

As long as the money you have in your bank account can be traced to your Social Security checks, that money cannot be attached for payment of debts.

But if you have spent money from your Social Security benefits, or any other source for that matter, the items you bought can still be attached. In other words, the store can repossess your television set if you fail to keep up your payments.

You should make some arrangements with the store to continue payments. Try to suggest that when you cannot make the full payment, you will make a partial payment. This will protect you from the store attempting to get back the television set.

Even your city or state government cannot attach your Social Security to get payment of bills you may owe them.

If your income is limited to Social Security benefits, you need to learn to budget carefully. It is not a good idea for people living on fixed incomes to buy things on time. You would be better off saving up for the television set before buying it. Don't forget that money in a savings account earns interest.

10. Can My Social Security Benefits Be Terminated?

DEAR MR. ANSWERMAN: What I would like to know is that now that I have applied for and gotten my Social Security benefits, can they ever be terminated? A friend of mine just had hers reduced after collecting for three years.

Janice B., Clifton, NJ

CONDITIONS FOR LOSS OF BENEFITS:

--Deportation
--Persons convicted of espionage
--Persons convicted of treason
--Convicted felons while in prison
--Aliens who are absent from the U.S. for more than six months
--Disability benefits when the person has recovered from the disability
--Receipt of benefits for a dependent child who is no longer living with recipient
--Divorced spouses who remarry
--Earning more than the allowable limit while collecting benefits

DEAR JANICE B: Since you did not tell me why your friend had her benefits reduced I cannot comment on her situation.

As far as you are concerned, you do not have to worry unless you fall into one of the special categories listed under your letter.

In most cases, the reduction or loss of benefits occurs when people receiving them earn more than the allowable limit when they are receiving benefits. This is something to be concerned about if you plan to continue working to any extent.

See Question 6 in Chapter I of this book for more detail on that issue.

The main thing to understand is that there is no absolute right to receive Social Security. Congress can establish conditions of eligibility for benefits and they are free to change these conditions. Usually, Congress has applied new rules only to new applicants.

Unless the conditions that Congress imposes on Social Security are unconstitutional or the Social Security Adminstration imposes conditions that are not authorized by Congress, then you must meet all the conditions of elibility to receive benefits.

A disabled person can lose benefits if he or she refuses rehabilitation services. If the disability is overcome, benefits will also be terminated.

And then certain criminals may have their benefits temorarily or permanently terminated. Aliens who receive benefits are usually required to not be out of the U.S. for more than six months.

DOCUMENTS CHART

Acceptable documents to submit for evidence are birth certificates, citizenship papers and marriage certificates. For a complete list of documents to use see Appendix III: Checklist of Essential Documents.

EVIDENCE TO BE SUBMITTED BY CLAIMANT[1]

Beneficiary	Age	Relationship			Dependency or support	School attendance	Child in care	Death of worker
		Marriage	Divorce	Parent-child				
Insured person[2]	X							
Spouse (62 or over)	X	X						
Spouse under 62 (child in care)		X		X			X	
Divorced spouse (62 or over)	X	X	X					
Child[2]	X			X	X	X		In survivor claims
Widow(er) (60 or over, 50 or over if disabled)[2]	X	X						X
Surviving divorced spouse[2]	X	X	X					X
Widow(er) under 62 or surviving divorced mother or father (child in care)		X	X	X			X	X
Parent	X			X	X			X
Lump sum:[6] A. Surviving spouse living in same household		X						X
B. Eligible surviving spouse, excluding divorced spouse	X	X						X
C. Eligible children	X			X	X	X		X

29

PC_____ REPORT OF MARRIAGE/DIVORCE

****
THIS IS NOT AN APPLICATION FOR A NEW SOCIAL SECURITY CARD IN YOUR NEW NAME.
YOU MUST FILL OUT AN APPLICATION FOR A NEW CARD.
****

YOUR NAME AS <u>CURRENTLY</u> SHOWN
ON SOCIAL SECURITY RECORDS: _____

YOUR SOCIAL SECURITY NUMBER: _____

SOCIAL SECURITY CLAIM NUMBER: _____ _____
                                                        Letter
****
<u>MARRIAGE</u>

DATE OF MARRIAGE: _____ CITY_____STATE_____

NEW NAME (IF APPLICABLE): _____

SPOUSE'S NAME: _____

SPOUSE'S SOCIAL SECURITY NUMBER: _____

DOES YOUR SPOUSE RECEIVE SOCIAL SECURITY BENEFITS: YES   NO

****
<u>DIVORCE</u>   # OF DIVORCE DECREE _____

DATE OF DIVORCE: _____ CITY_____STATE_____

NEW NAME (IF APPLICABLE): _____

DIVORCED SPOUSE'S NAME: _____

DIVORCED SPOUSE'S SOCIAL SESCURITY NUMBER: _____

DOES YOUR DIVORCED SPOUSE RECEIVE SOCIAL SECURITY BENEFITS: YES NO

****
IF WE DETERMINE THAT A CERTIFIED COPY OF YOUR MARRIAGE CERTIFICATE OR DIVORCE
DECREE IS NEEDED, WE WILL CONTACT YOU AT A LATER DATE.
****

CURRENT MAILING ADDRESS: _____

_____

CURRENT DAY TIME PHONE NUMBER: _____

SIGNATURE:_____DATE:_____
Revised November 1, 1990

30

REQUEST FOR BENEFIT RECOMPUTATION

****

NAME:_____

SOCIAL SECURITY NUMBER:_____

****

I REQUEST MY SOCIAL SECURITY BENEFITS BE RECOMPUTED TO INCLUDE MY EARNINGS FOR

_____.
        Year

I HAVE ATTACHED A COPY OF MY W-2 FORM FOR _____.
                                                  Year

(The W-2 will be returned by mail.)

****

CURRENT MAILING ADDRESS:_____

_____

YOUR DAY TIME PHONE NUMBER:_____

****

_____   _____
            SIGNATURE   DATE

Revised December 13, 1990

REQUEST FOR VERIFICATION OF BENEFITS

****

NAME:_____ _____ _____
          FIRST   MIDDLE INITIAL   LAST

YOUR SOCIAL SECURITY NUMBER:_____

SOCIAL SECURITY CLAIM NUMBER:_____ _____
                                                                         Letter

****

I REQUEST A VERIFICATION OF MY:

        ( ) SOCIAL SECURITY BENEFITS

        ( ) SUPPLEMENTAL SECURITY INCOME BENEFITS (SSI)

THE VERIFICATION SHOULD INCLUDE THE FOLLOWING PERSONS:

      NAME:_____SSN:_____

      NAME:_____SSN:_____

      NAME:_____SSN:_____

      NAME:_____SSN:_____

****

TO WHOM/WHERE DO YOU WANT THIS INFORMATION SENT?

                      _____

                      _____

                      _____

YOUR DAY TIME PHONE NUMBER:_____

****

_____ _____
             SIGNATURE   DATE
Revised November 1, 1990

START/STOP WORK NOTICE
FOR
SOCIAL SECURITY RETIREMENT/SURVIVORS BENEFITS
****

NAME: _____ , _____
                    Last Name   First Name

SOCIAL SECURITY CLAIM NUMBER: _____ _____
                                                                 Letter
****

STARTING WORK

DATE YOU   AMOUNT YOU EXPECT
STARTED WORK:_____   TO EARN THIS YEAR:_____
                                                  GROSS WAGES

CIRCLE EACH MONTH YOU EXPECT TO EARN LESS THAN $590 (IF YOU ARE UNDER 65)
OR $810 (IF YOU ARE 65 OR OLDER IN 1990) IN GROSS WAGES:

    JAN   FEB   MAR   APR   MAY   JUN   JUL   AUG   SEP   OCT   NOV   DEC

DO YOU PLAN TO CONTINUE WORKING NEXT YEAR?   YES   NO

IF YES, WHAT ARE YOUR ESTIMATED GROSS WAGES FOR NEXT YEAR? $_____

****

STOPPING WORK

DATE YOU   AMOUNT YOU
STOPPED WORK:_____   EARNED THIS YEAR:_____
                                                  GROSS WAGES

CIRCLE EACH MONTH YOU EARNED LESS THAN $570 (IF YOU ARE UNDER 65)
OR $780 (IF YOU ARE 65 OR OLDER IN 1990) IN GROSS WAGES:

    JAN   FEB   MAR   APR   MAY   JUN   JUL   AUG   SEP   OCT   NOV   DEC

****

CURRENT MAILING ADDRESS: _____

_____

CURRENT DAY TIME PHONE NUMBER: _____

_____   _____
             SIGNATURE   DATE
Revised November 1, 1990

CHANGE OF ADDRESS
FOR
SOCIAL SECURITY CHECKS

*********************PLEASE COMPLETE THE INFORMATION BELOW*******************

YOUR CLAIM NUMBER:_____   _____
                                                              Letter

YOUR NAME:_____ , _____
                     Last Name   First Name

YOUR OLD ADDRESS: _____

ZIP CODE: _____

YOUR NEW ADDRESS: _____

ZIP CODE: _____

EFFECTIVE MONTH OF CHANGE: _____

TELEPHONE NUMBER: (__) _____

******YOUR SOCIAL SECURITY NUMBER: _____ ******

DO YOUR CHECKS GO DIRECTLY TO THE BANK: YES   NO

IF YES, DO YOU WANT THEM TO CONTINUE TO THE BANK: YES   NO

IF NO, DO YOU WANT TO START THEM TO THE BANK: YES   NO

BANK ROUTING NUMBER_____ACCOUNT NUMBER_____

WHAT IS YOUR DATE OF BIRTH?   _____

ARE THERE ANY OTHER FAMILY MEMBERS WHO
RECEIVE BENEFITS FROM THIS SOCIAL SECURITY RECORD?   YES   NO

IF YES, LIST THEIR NAMES AND THEIR SOCIAL SECURITY NUMBERS BELOW:

_____   _____

_____   _____
      YOUR SIGNATURE   DATE

ℸℸℸ
IT WILL TAKE APPROXIMATELY 60 DAYS FOR YOUR ADDRESS TO CHANGE SO
PLEASE LEAVE A FORWARDING ADDRESS WITH THE POST OFFICE.

IF YOU RECEIVE SSI YOU MAY NEED TO SEE SOMEONE/MAKE AN APPOINTMENT
REVISED NOVEMBER 1, 1990

REPORT OF DEATH

****

THIS IS NOT AN APPLICATION FOR SURVIVOR'S BENEFITS. YOU MUST FILE AN APPLICATION

****

NAME OF DECEASED BENEFICIARY:_____

SOCIAL SECURITY CLAIM NUMBER:_____ _____

Letter

DATE OF DEATH:_____

CITY AND STATE WHERE DEATH OCCURRED:_____

WAS THE DECEASED BENEFICIARY MARRIED AT THE TIME OF DEATH?   YES   NO

SPOUSE'S NAME:_____

SPOUSE'S SOCIAL SECURITY NUMBER:_____

SPOUSE'S DATE OF BIRTH:_____

SPOUSE'S ADDRESS:_____

_____

SPOUSE'S DAY TIME PHONE NUMBER:_____

****

WE WILL NEED TO SEE A CERTIFIED COPY OF THE DEATH CERTIFICATE. IF
YOU HAVE ONE, PLEASE ATTACH IT TO THIS FORM. IT WILL BE MAILED
BACK TO YOU IMMEDIATELY. IF YOU DO NOT HAVE A CERTIFIED COPY OF
THE DEATH CERTIFICATE, PLEASE TAKE AN ENVELOPE AND MAIL IT WHEN
RECEIVED (IT WILL BE MAILED BACK TO YOU IMMEDIATELY).

****

YOUR NAME:_____

YOUR CURRENT MAILING ADDRESS:_____

_____

YOUR DAY TIME PHONE NUMBER:_____

****

_____   _____
                SIGNATURE   DATE
Revised November 1, 1990

III: KNOWING MORE ABOUT SSI

1. What Is SSI?

DEAR MR. ANSWERMAN: My friends and I have been arguing over the purpose of SSI. My friend Dave says that it is extra income from Social Security if you have contributed heavily to the benefits during your working years.

But my friend Walt disagrees. He says that SSI means reduced benefits. And Abe says that they are both wrong. He says that SSI is for people who have special problems, but he doesn't know what those problems are.

Can you straighten us out? If there is something there that we could qualify for, we sure would like to know. All of us are currently collecting Social Security.

Al P. and Co., Boulder, CO

IN BRIEF:

--SSI is administered by the Social Security Administration.
--It is funded from general tax revenues.
--SSI is the first federally administered cash assistance program in this country that is available to the general public.
--Its purpose is to provide an income base for the aged, blind, or disabled who have little or no income or resources.
--You may have some income and property and still qualify for SSI.

DEAR AL P: You and your company of friends all need a little more information about SSI, I can see. Your friend Abe came closest to the truth. It is a special benefit program.

The Federal government had two objectives in establishing SSI benefits:

ONE: To transfer to the Federal rolls those who had previously received Federal-State assistance payments as aged, blind, or disabled persons.

TWO: To establish a new uniform national program for payment to the aged, blind, or disabled.

SSI stands for Supplemental Security Income. It pays monthly checks to those who qualify for these benefits. People on SSI are not necessarily over 65. Some SSI recipients are children who are blind or disabled, or young adults in the same categories.

Even though there are a large number of individuals currently getting SSI benefits, there are still estimated to be many more who qualify but have not applied for benefits.

SSI has been a successful program, giving low-income people in these special categories cash assistance to help them maintain a decent standard of living. SSI benefits also qualify a person for Medicaid.

2. Who Qualifies For SSI?

DEAR MR. ANSWERMAN: I know that SSI benefits are meant for the disabled, the blind, or the aged who need money to live on. How can my neighbor collect SSI on top of her Social Security, when she is not blind or disabled?

Suzanne M., Anchorage, AK

IN BRIEF:

--Those aged 65 or older in need may claim SSI
--A legally blind person who has vision that is no better than 20/200 even with glasses or who has tunnel vision, or limited peripheral vision may claim SSI
--A person who is physically or mentally disabled and is thereby prevented from do any substantial work may claim SSI
--The claimant must be a resident of the United States
--The claimant must be a citizen or a legal alien
--Claimant does not have countable income in a month of more than the amount of the Federal benefit rate for an individual or for a couple, if that is applicable in a case
--Has limited countable resources determined by Social Security
--SSI uses a means test to qualify people for benefits

DEAR SUZANNE M: It is not always obvious why a person qualifies for SSI benefits. You would need to know more about the individual to know exactly how the person does qualify.

To get SSI you have to be either 65 "or" blind "or" disabled.

Blind does not necessarily mean totally blind. It can mean extremely poor vision. Children, as well as adults, are eligible to collect SSI because of blindness.

Children, as well as adults, can also claim SSI benefits because of a disability. Disability covers both physical disability and mental problems.

When people file for SSI they are asked to give the names and addresses of doctors and medical treatment facilities, the dates of treatment and any other information that might relate to the situation. Claims do have to be verified with medical evidence.

Claimants also are asked to furnish pertinent information about their activities before and after the onset of the disability to determine their ability to work.

This is the medical evidence that SSI asks for:
 * A report signed by a licensed doctor
 * A copy or abstract of the medical records
 * Any other available medical evidence, such as treatment, tests, findings, and other information to support the claim

It is unlikely that your neighbor is collecting SSI benefits and is not eligible. While SSI is a humane program, it does not give benefits to just anyone who asks for them. A legitimate need must first be established.

3. How Much Can I Get From SSI?

DEAR MR. ANSWERMAN: I thought that everyone who is collecting SSI benefits got the same amount of money. But recently I learned that an uncle of mine who lives in another state is collecting more in SSI benefits than my mother who lives with me. Can you please expain how benefits are determined and why one person would get more than another one?

It doesn't seem quite fair to me. I think my mother's needs are even greater than my uncle's. He certainly lives in a better house and even has a car.

Marvin C., Gallup, NM

SOME FACTORS THAT DETERMINE SSI BENEFIT AMOUNTS:

--*Receiving Worker's Compensation*
--*Receiving a benefit as a widow or widower of a disabled person*
--*State benefits*
--*Local or State laws*
--*The date of the disability onset*
--*The date entitlement began*
--*Work performed during disability*
--*Lump-sum settlements from insurers*
--*Lump-sum agreements from employers*
--*Living arrangements*

DEAR MARVIN C: There are a number of factors involved in determining what a disabled, aged, or blind person's monthly benefit payment will be. I have listed some of them under your letter in the left-hand column.

The basic SSI check for a single person is $407 a month. The basic check for a couple is $610 a month. But a person may get a lot more if the State in which he or she lives adds money to the basic check. Or the claimant may receive less if there is other monies coming into the household.

In the case of your uncle and mother, one or more of these situations may be working in your uncle's favor.

The first monthly SSI check may be for less than for a full month, because the person is paid only for the days since the person applied for SSI. By the second month a full check will be received.

Some benefits a disabled person may be receiving are excluded from reducing an SSI claim. Among them are:

* Veterans benefits
* Federal benefits based on employment covered by Social Security
* Needs-based benefits
* Private pensions
* Insurance benefits

You might want to explore your mother's situation with Social Security or your local adult protective services agency. There is a list of Aging and Adult Administration agencies in the Appendix of this book. Contact the one in your state for more information or a referral.

CHART FOR FIGURING REDUCED BENEFITS

Explanation of abbreviations: RIB = retirement (old-age) insurance benefit; PIA = primary insurance amount; SIB = spouse's (wife's or husband's) insurance benefit; WIB = widow's or widower's insurance benefit; DIB = disability insurance benefit; RA:R = reduction amount for RIB; RA:S = reduction amount for SIB; RA:W = reduction amount for WIB; RA:D = reduction amount for DIB; Months: 65 = number of months before age 65 (but not before age 60); Months: 62 = number of months before age 62 (but not before age 60); Months: = number of months before age 60; RA:INC = increase in reduction amount for RIB; RA:W(F) = fictional reduction amount for WIB.

Case No.	Entitlement to		Example		Formulas for reduction amounts and reduced benefits	Example of computation	Benefit payable	Payable from age
1	RIB	before age 65	PIA	$189.00 age 62	PIA x 1/180 x Months:65 = RA:R PIA – RA:R = Reduced RIB	$189.00 x 1/180 x 36 = $37.80 $189 – $37.80 = $151.20	$151.20	62
2	SIB	before age 65	SIB	$94.50 age 62	SIB x 1/144 x Months:65 = RA:S SIB – RA:S = Reduced SIB	$94.50 x 1/144 x 36 = $23.60 $94.50 – $23.60 = $70.90	$70.90	62
3	WIB	before age 65 (age 60 or later)*	WIB	$189.00 age 60	WIB x 19/4000 x Months:65 = RA:W WIB – RA:W = Reduced WIB	$189.00 x 19/4000 x 60 = $53.80 $189.00 – $53.80 = $135.20	$135.20	60
4	WIB	before age 60	WIB	$189.00 age 50	(WIB x 19/4000 x Months:65) = RA:W WIB – RA:W = Reduced WIB	($189.00 x 19/4000 x 60) = $53.80 $189.00 – $53.80 = $135.20	$135.20	50
5	RIB	before age 65 and larger SIB simultaneously	PIA SIB	$123.10 age 62 $137.90 age 62	PIA – RA:R = Reduced RIB (same formula as Case 1) (SIB – PIA) x 1/144 x Months:65=RA:S SIB – PIA – 62 RA:S = Reduced Net SIB	$123.10 – $24.60 = $98.50 ($137.90 – $123.10) x 1/144 x 36 = $3.70 $137.90 – $123.10 – $3.70 = $11.10	$98.50 +$11.10	62 62
6	RIB	before age 65 and larger SIB at age 65 or later	PIA SIB	$123.10 age 62 $137.90 age 65	PIA – RA:R = Reduced RIB (same formula as Case 1) SIB – PIA = Net SIB	$123.10 – $24.60 = $98.50 $137.90 – $123.10 = $14.80	$98.50 +$14.80	62 65
7	RIB	before age 65 and subsequent entitlement to DIB	PIA DIB	$189.00 age 62 $189.00 age 63	PIA – RA:R = Reduced RIB (Case 1) PIA x 1/180 x Months:65** = RA:D DIB – RA:D = Reduced DIB	$189.00 – $37.80 = $151.20 $189.00 x 1/180 x 12 = $12.60 $189.00 – $12.60 = $176.40	$151.20 $176.40	62 63
8	SIB	before age 65 and smaller RIB later but before age 65	SIB PIA	$137.90 age 62 $114.30 age 63	SIB – RA:S = Reduced SIB (Case 2) PIA – RA:R = Reduced RIB (same formula as Case 1) Reduced SIB – Reduced RIB = Net SIB	$137.90 – $34.40 = $103.50 $114.30 – $15.20 = $99.10 $103.50 – $99.10 = $4.40	$103.50 $99.10 + $4.40	62 63 63
9	RIB	before age 65 and increase in PIA before age 65	PIA PIA	$176.10 age 62 $186.50 age 63	PIA – RA:R = Reduced RIB (Case 1) New PIA – RA:R*** = Reduced RIB	$176.10 – $35.20 = $140.90 $186.50 x 1/180 x 36 = $37.30	$140.90 $149.20	62 63
10	WIB	before age 65 and RIB at age 65 or later*	WIB PIA	$139.40 age 60 $114.30 age 65	WIB – RA:W = Reduced WIB (Case 3) WIB x 19/4000 x Months:62 = RA:W(F) PIA – RA:W(F) = Reduced RIB Reduced WIB – Reduced RIB = Net Reduced WIB	$139.40 – $39.70 = $99.70 $139.40 x 19/4000 x 24 = $15.90 $114.30 – $15.90 = $98.40 $99.70 – $98.40 = $1.30	$99.70 $98.40 + $1.30	60 65 65
11	WIB	before age 65 and RIB at age 65 or later*	WIB PIA	$139.40 age 60 $120.00 age 65	WIB – RA:W = Reduced WIB (Case 3) WIB x 19/4000 x Months:62 = RA:W(F) PIA – RA:W(F) = Reduced RIB Reduced WIB – Reduced RIB = Net Reduced WIB (cannot be less than $0.00)	$139.40 – $39.70 = $99.70 $139.40 x 19/4000 x 24 = $15.90 $120.00 – $15.90 = $104.10 $99.70 – $104.10 = $0.00	$99.70 $104.10 + $0.00	60 65 65

*Spouse had not received a reduced benefit.

39

4. How Can I Get Other Help?

DEAR MR. ANSWERMAN: I have been collecting SSI benefits for about a year and a half and I am really having a hard time making ends meet. I'm afraid if I can't keep up with my monthly rent, I'll end up out on the street like a lot of homeless people I see today wandering around some parts of our town.

I always make sure the rent is paid first, but sometimes there just isn't enough left over for food and lately I have been skipping some meals. I don't have any relatives to turn to for help. Can you please give my some ideas of how I could more help to meet my basic needs?

Ronald S., High Point, NC

CHART SHOWING AN ADJUSTMENT OF BENFIT RATES FOR FAMILY COVERAGE:

	Original benefit	Adjusted for the maximum	Adjustment when benefits not payable to one child	Adjustment when benefits not payable to two children
Insured person	$300.60	$300.60	$300.60	$300.60
Spouse	150.30	58.70	78.20	117.30
First child	150.30	58.70	78.20	117.30
Second child	150.30	58.70	78.20	0.00
Third child	150.30	58.70	0.00	0.00
Total	$901.80	$535.40	$535.20	$535.20

Note that the total benefits payable to the family group are not necessarily reduced when monthly benefits are not payable to one member of the family group.

DEAR RONALD S: Times are tough, I know. There is some other help you can get if you are on SSI. You may also be able to get help from your State, County, or City government.

You may be able to qualify for food stamps which will certainly help you to get more food for your basic needs. You should also check to see if there are any meal services run by charitable agencies where you could go for lunch or dinner at certain regular times. All these can help you get the nutrition you need, and if you are living alone, you will get out and socialize with other people. This is important because it can help you keep your spirits up.

Your Social Security office or your local food stamp office can help you sign up for food stamps. Besides food stamps, you may also qualify for Medicaid to help you with your health needs, doctor and hospital bills, and medicine. Check into this at your local welfare or medical assistance office.

Some other sources of help are through utility companies. In many communities, the electric and gas companies have programs to help those in need pay for their utility bills. These are usually funded through private donations by the consumers in the area. People donate as little as a dollar a month into these programs when they pay their utility bill each month. That may not sound like a lot, but when you multiply it by the number of households paying one dollar, the monthly sum is enough to help many disabled people who are need of help.

5. How Much Income Can I Have And Still Collect SSI?

DEAR MR. ANSWERMAN: I am in the process of applying for SSI benefits. At present I am getting some help from my family and from my church until the benefits begin. Will the help I am getting reduce my benefits?

I also hope in a few months to be able to do some part-time work and was wondering how that might cut into my monthly check. Can you help me with these questions?

Carol M., Biloxi, MS

WHAT SSI DOESN'T COUNT TO DETERMINE BENEFITS:

--The first $65 a month you earn and half of the amount over $65
--Food stamps
--Food, clothing, or shelter from a private non-profit organization
--Home energy assistance
--Some wages or scholarships of students
--Wages used to pay for items or services needed because of your disability
--Wages used to pay for special services to enable the claimant to work
--Income used for special training to enable the claimant to work

DEAR CAROL M: I doubt very much if any of the considerations you are getting from your family or your church will be used to reduce your benefits under SSI.

Let's define what is meant by income, so that you can better understand how Social Security makes a determination for someone to collect SSI benefits.

Income is the money you receive as wages, Social Security checks, and pensions. Income also includes non-cash items you receive such as food, clothing, or shelter.

Social Security also looks at the income of spouses in the case of a married person seeking benefits. They will want to know what the spouse's income is and the things that person owns.

The amount of income you can have each month and still get SSI depends in part on where you live. You can usually get SSI if your income is less that $427 in all States. For a couple the benefit is $630. What each State allows does differ from State to State.

At the back of this book there is an appendix that lists the regional offices of Social Security, along with their phone numbers.

If you cannot get the information you need from your local agency, feel free to contact them. Please remember that the best time to call Social Security for information is in the latter half of the week and after the first week of the month. You have a much better chance of getting through the telephone lines at that time.

6. How Much Can I Own And Still Get SSI?

DEAR MR. ANSWERMAN: I recently had an accident at work and injured my back. It appears that I will be disabled for at least six months, maybe even as much as a year and a half, according to my doctors.

I am just getting around to applying for SSI benefits, but I am concerned that I will be denied them because I own my home and have some other assets. Will Social Security turn me down or ask me to sell off my assets before I can collect SSI benefits?

Jackson H., Rochester, NY

EXCLUDED RESOURCES:

--Your home, adjacent land, and buildings on the property that you or your spouse owns
--Household goods
--Personal effects
--Personal items needed because of your physical condition
--Self-support property, like tools, equipment, vehicles
--Real property, investment property used in the operation of a business
--Your automobile
--Life insurance policies with a total face value of $1500 or less
--Replacement of an excludable resource by insurance after a major disaster
--Assets needed to accomplish a plan to achieve self-support
--Burial spaces and funds up to $1500, plus accrued interest, is excluded

DEAR JACKSON H: You do not have to worry. Your house will be excluded and if you review the list of exclusions I have placed under your letter, you will be able to decide if your other assets are also excludable.

Social Security considers items like real estate, personal belongsins, bank accounts, cash, stocks, and bonds as things you own. A person may get SSI benefits with items worth up to $2000 and a couple can have $3000 worth of items that they own.

But there are many exclusions that you may own, which Social Security does not count.

Some of your liquid resources, which are defined as assets that are immediately available, are counted. But items like savings bonds or savings certificates are not considered available until they mature.

Excess resources are those which are not needed to provide for basic needs. If you have these resources, you may be asked to convert them to liquid assets. Three months for person property and six months for real property is the usual time frame, but extensions can be made if you can show that you have made a real effort to dispose of excess property you may have.

For instance, you might have an extra subdivided lot next to the house you live in. You may try to sell it, but the real estate market conditions may be very sluggish and you cannot sell the property. As long as you keep it on the market and attempt to sell it, Social Security will exclude it.

7. What Are The Residency Requirements For SSI?

DEAR MR. ANSWERMAN: I have been collecting SSI benefits and am thinking about moving to a warmer climate, like the Bahamas. Will this affect my ability to collect SSI and Social Security benefits?

Henry G., Washington, DC

RESIDENCY IN BRIEF:

--*You must live in the United States or Northern Mariana Islands*
--*You must be a citizen or legal resident*
--*You may receive both Social Security and SSI benefits*
--*Residents who live in city or county rest homes, halfway house, or other public institutions usually cannot get SSI, although there may be exceptions*
--*Residents of publicly operated community residences that serve no more than 16 people may get SSI*
--*Residence in a public institution during an approved educational or job training program usually qualifies for SSI*
--*Those living in public emergency shelters for the homeless may be eligible to get SSI*
--*Residents in public or private institutions when more than half the cost is paid by Medicaid may get SSI*

DEAR HENRY G: If you move to the Bahamas, you will lose your SSI benefit, but not your Social Security.

Persons outside the United States for a full month or more are not eligible for those benefits for such months. A person who has been outside the United States for 30 consecutive days does not become eligible again until he or she is back in the United States for 30 consecutive days.

Your SSI benefits can also be affected by your living arrangements. Federal SSI benefits are reduced by one-third if you are living in the household of another person and receiving support and maintenance.

Living in an institution may also affect your benefits. For instance, prisoners and residents of mental hospitals are not eligible for SSI benefits at all.

In cases where you are hospitalized and Medicaid is paying for more than 50 percent of your care, you will only receive $30 per month from SSI.

Sometimes residents of nonmedical retirement homes may receive more than if they were living alone because of the costs involved in living in those institutions.

Your SSI is also affected by the State in which you live. Some States have their own plans to add to SSI benefits.

8. How Do I Sign Up For SSI?

DEAR MR. ANSWERMAN: I need to sign up for SSI benefits. I am already on Social Security. My doctor says that my vision is so bad that I should also be collecting SSI benefits to help me deal with the difficulties I have getting from place to place.

Because my sight is so bad, it is hard for me to know what documents I need to apply for SSI benefits. Are they the same as for Social Security? Since I am already on Social Security, can't they use the documents I submitted for retirement benefits?

Ken H., Manchester, NH

REPORTING CHANGES TO SSI:

--Change in work
--Change in residence
--Marriage, divorce, or separation
--Absence from the United State
--Improvement in disability condition
--Change in income
--Change in resources
--Eligibility for other benefits
--Change in school attendance
--Change in household composition

It is necessary to report the above changes to SSI when collecting benefits. Failure to do so may result in a penalty. First time penalty is $25. Penalties are not assessed if the person was without fault or had good cause for failure to report.

DEAR KEN H: It is easy to sign up for SSI. Just visit your local Social Security office or call 1-800-772-1213 for an appointment with a Social Security representative to help you sign up.

You should apply for SSI right away. Don't wait to find your papers. If anything is missing, you can find them while your application is being processed. SSI can start from the day that you apply, so it is important to apply as soon as possible.

For children under the age of 18, their parents or guardians can apply for them.

Here is a list of things you will need to apply:

* Your Social Security card or number
* Your birth certificate or other proof of age
* Information about the home in which you live, such as you landlord's name, your lease, or mortgage information
* Payroll slips, bank books, insurance policies, car registration, burial fund records, and any other information about your income and the things you own
* For disability, you need the names and addresses of doctors, hospitals, and clinics that have seen you
* Names and addresses of social workers or institutions that have aided you

Even if you do not have all the things you need, sign up anyway. The people in the Social Security office can help you get whatever is needed to process your claim.

Bring your checkbook account number if you want your checks deposited directly into your bank account.

9. Can I Work Part-Time And Collect SSI?

DEAR MR. ANSWERMAN: My husband and I are both working part-time and collecting Social Security benefits. He recently was advised that he is eligible to collect SSI because of his heart condition.

We would like to apply for the SSI benefit and still go on working part-time, if possible. We want to review carefully how we can meet all our financial needs and to calculate if we would be better off collecting SSI.

If it means that either of us has to stop working part-time, we would not be too happy about that. We still feel that working gives us a great sense of independence and makes us still feel useful.

We have seen too many of our friends and acquaintances wither up like dried leaves when they stop working entirely.

Can you give us some information to help us decide what to do?

Elizabeth T., Honolulu, HI

EARNED INCOME DEFINED:

--Wages paid for services as an employee
--Net earnings from self-employment estimated for a current year based on the volume of business and past experience
--Payments for services performed in a sheltered workshp or work activities center
--Payments on account of earned income credits, as provisions of the IRS

DEAR ELIZABETH T: Your attitude toward work is commendable. It looks like there are more and more retired citizens who want to keep on working and this country certainly needs experienced workers who have such a positive attitude as yours and your husband's.

To be eligible for Federal SSI benefits, your countable monthly income cannot exceed $354 for a single person or $532 for a couple.

You will need some guidance on this question from Social Security. Remember some States supplement SSI by paying additional benefits. This might complicate your claim.

Social Security will consider all your income when you make an SSI claim. This means that they will consider cash or in kind that you receive to meet your needs for food, clothing, or shelter. They will consider "in-kind" income, which means non-cash benefits for food and clothing.

There are many kinds of income that Social Security excludes. See Question 6 on page 42 for a list of EXCLUDED RESOURCES that will not be counted against you.

Determining how much income you are receiving is the key to deciding whether your husband is eligible for Federal SSI benefits. Get an evaluation at your local Social Security office before you decide to apply. If it looks like it would be possible for you to receive the benefits and work part-time, do so. If you are turned down, you still have a right to appeal, if you think you are entitled to benefits.

10. What Is The SSI Appeal Process?

DEAR MR. ANSWERMAN: Recently, I was turned down by Social Security for SSI benefits, even though I have become totally unable to work because of a serious diabetes condition.

I feel the problem comes because they have counted income that should have been excluded. I have decided to appeal the decision. Can you review the process for me, so that I know what to expect along the way?

Keith A., Lincoln, NB

NONCOUNTABLE INCOME TO DETERMINE SSI ELIGIBILITY:

—*Income-tax refunds*

—*Property-tax refunds*

—*Food-sales-tax refunds*

—*Medicare Part B premium paid by an insurance company or Medicaid*

—*Wages from VISTA and other recognized paid programs, like Foster Grandparents*

—*Certain foster care payments*

—*Family consumed home produce*

—*Free meals under Title 7*

—*Medical care*

—*Noncash social services*

—*Need based State or local government payments*

—*Federal housing assistance*

—*Private nonprofit support or maintenance assistance*

—*Small amounts ($10) of infrequent earned income*

DEAR KEITH A: First let me say that you cannot collect if you are employed, but I'm glad you asked about the appeal process. It is similar to the one in Social Security with some differences. It pays to review them before beginning the process.

INITIAL DETERMINATION: These are decisions to grant or deny an application, as well as decisions to reduce, suspend, or terminate benefits. You must appeal an adverse initial determination, otherwise it will become final.

RECONSIDERATION: File a request for "reconsideration" within sixty days of receipt of the "initial determination." Use an SSA form or your own letter. Social Security will acknowledge receipt of your request and schedule the "reconsideration." There are three methods:

Case Review: You can submit additional evidence and discuss your situation with an SSA employee.

Informal Conference: You can bring witnesses and an SSA employee will keep a record of the conference for your file.

Formal Conference: Documents and witnesses can be subpoenaed. You may cross examine witnesses. A record will be kept in your file.

Choose the method that is best for your situation. If you appeal determinations to suspend, reduce, or terminate your SSI benefits within ten days, your benefits will continue until a decision is made.

IV: WHAT YOU SHOULD KNOW ABOUT PRIVATE PENSIONS

1. What Do I Need To Know About My Company's Pension Plan?

DEAR MR. ANSWERMAN: I have been working for a major electronics company for several years. While I have been promoted and received bonuses for my work, I'm still not sure about the exact details of the company's retirement plan.

Who should I see to get specific information and what are some of the important questions I should ask?

Monica P., Monroe, LA

MAJOR QUESTIONS TO ASK ABOUT PENSION PLANS:

—*How long do I have to be employed before I am covered by the plan?*

—*At what age do I become eligible for benefits?*

—*Do I have an early retirement option?*

—*Do I have a choice about monthly or lump sum payments?*

—*Does the plan offer life or health insurance? If so, does it continue after I retire?*

—*What will my dependents get when I die?*

—*How much will I receive? Will it affect my Social Security benefits?*

—*How and when should I apply for benefits? Whom should I contact?*

DEAR MONICA P: Each employer is required by law to furnish information to employees that explains the pension plan. It is wise to meet with your employer's pension plan administrator, benefits counselor, or personnel representative for a complete explanation of the plan's benefits. It is best to do this long before you are ready to retire, so that you can plan accordingly.

The law requires that each employee may request the receipt of an annual statement of credits that have accumulated to enable the employee to determine his or her approximate retirement benefits.

Ask how your company's plan is funded and the way the benefits are formulated. Most pension plans are funded by employer contributions, while others are funded by employer and employee contributions.

It is your responsibility to learn everything you can about your pension benefits, since your future economic security is dependent upon it and your Social Security benefits.

Unfortunately, most pension plans do not have automatic cost-of-living provisions for inflation, but some companies do offer periodic increases to pension benefits. Eligibility requirements vary widely among employers, but the law was changed in 1989 to require shorter periods of work to qualify for benefits.

2. What Is Vesting?

DEAR MR. ANSWERMAN: I just spoke to the personnel manager of our company's retirement plan. He said that our plan has a "5 year cliff" schedule for our vesting standard.

Can you explain what that means and how it is different from a "graded vesting" schedule which my husband has with his company?

Nan W., Silver Spring, MD

VESTING STANDARDS:

--*"5 year cliff" means that the participant is eligible for the employer-provided benefit upon the completion of five years of service.*
--*"Graded vesting" schedules provide that an employee is elibible to the employer-provided benefit with 20 percent vesting after 3 years and increases by 20 percent increments each year until 100 percent vesting is reached after 7 years of participation.*
--*Employees are 100 percent vested in their own contributions*
--*IRS sometimes requires faster vesting for rank and file workders if the company retirement plan benefits higher paid employees or owners of the business.*

DEAR NAN W: Simply put, vesting rules tell how long you have to work for an employer before you can collect a pension at retirement.

Vesting rules vary from employer to employer, but you usually have to work for an employer for 10 years. People who move frequently from job to job, might not have any vested pension benefits. If the person quits work before being vested, he or she gets back only the contributions paid into the system by the employee and none that was paid by the employer.

Beginning in 1989, however, employers were required to adopt one of two vesting standards. The "5 year cliff" schedule and the "graded-vesting" schedule are explained under your letter.

While many more work-ers will now earn vested benefits, the pension benefits based on short service early in one's career will not likely be worth very much. This is because they are usually based on salary at the time of job separation, with no adjustment made for inflation.

Of course, one could argue that the "graded-vesting" schedule has the advantage of 20 percent vesting after 3 years. Those who do a lot of job hopping might do slightly better with this method.

You might want to ask your personnel manager how your company's retirement plan works if you take a leave of absence and then return to work.

The main point about retirement plans is that you keep informed about it. Pay attention to any literature your company has or puts out in the future.

3. What Is ERISA?

DEAR MR. ANSWERMAN: I am a small businessman trying to set up a pension plan for my company.

I have about 15 employees, including myself. I would like to offer some of my employees a pension benefit plan along with a health plan.

I understand that there is a government act that supervises rules and regulations about pension plans.

Is there any literature that I can get on this subject? What is this act called? I would appreciate any information you can give me on this subject.

Mitch M., Gary, IN

LAWS THAT REGULATE PRIVATE PENSION PLANS:

--ERISA (Employee Retirement Income Security Act of 1974
--Labor Management Relations Act
--Age Discrimination in Employment Act of 1967
--Civil Rights Act of 1964
--Internal Revenue Code
--Welfare and Pension Plans Disclosure Act of 1958
--National Labor Relations Board decision of 1948
--Revenue Act of 1942
--Revenue Act of 1926 and 1921

DEAR MR. SMALL BUSINESSMAN MITCH M: The act you are referring to is ERISA, the Employee Retirement Income Security Act. You can get more detailed information about ERISA from your local office of the U.S. Department of Labor.

This act came about because of abuse and mismanagement in the private pension system. Employers were taking tax deductions for their contributions to pension plans, but many employees were not receiving the pensions they thought they were paying into.

The requirements before ERISA went into effect often denied pensions to employees because they failed to meet the length of service requirements or the companies simply went out of business.

Prior to ERISA, the Internal Revenue Code regulated private pension plans by granting them a tax-qualified status to deduct the pension trust contributions from being taxed.

ERISA regulates plans by employers engaged in commerce, industry, or employee organizations that represent those engaged in these activities. ERISA also regulates qualified tax-favored plans.

ERISA does not regulate government plans, church plans, fraternal organization plans, plans outside the U.S., welfare plans, unfunded excess benefit plans, nor unfunded, nonqualified deferred compensation plans for select groups of top managment or highly paid executives.

It is wise for you to discuss your pension plans with your CPA and your attorney before implementing it.

4. Should I Receive My Pension In A Lump Sum Or Monthly Payments?

DEAR MR. ANSWERMAN: I am approaching retirement soon. The benefits manager of my company has been explaining that I can take the lump sum or monthly payment plan when I retire. I'm not too sure that I understand the benefits of the two approaches.

It would help me if you could tell me what some of my major considerations should be on making a decisions in this choice. Can you give me some guidelines?

Helen G., Grand Forks, ND

MAJOR CONSIDERATIONS:

--Is a monthly check critical to your daily needs?
--Will your private pension plan income be disposable income?
--Are you comfortable managing and investing large sums of money that the lump-sum payment would give you?
--Your family history regarding longevity and health is a consideration. If your family history and health suggest that you will live a long life, the monthly annuity amount might be more advantageous.

DEAR HELEN G: Workers are given the option of collecting their pension in monthly payments, called an annuity, or collecting a fixed amount at retirement in a one-time payment, called a lump sum.

Pension annuities are usually guaranteed for life. Depending on how long you live, you could receive more through a lump sum payment than through an annuity.

If you decide on a lump sum payment, you have to consider how much income tax you will owe if you take this option. You also have to be a good money manager and should understand something about making large investments.

You do have the option of rolling over your lump sum payment into an IRA within 60 days after receipt. This way you can take regular installments and only pay tax on that part that you use as income.

Take a careful look at your company's pension plan to see if it only pays benefits for your lifetime or if it has joint and survivor benefits, which pays benefits to you and one other person.

Other types of plans might pay benefits for your lifetime and for a guaranteed period of time, say ten years. Your beneficiary can then receive them in the case of your death.

Another type of plan pays a stated amount for a definite number of installments. For example, the amount may be $90,000 paid out in 120 equal monthly payments. When 10 years have passed the payments end.

5. Are Survivors Protected Under Private Pension Plans?

DEAR MR. ANSWERMAN: Considering the amount of money that I am setting aside for my company pension plan, I would like to know what happens to the money if I should die before my spouse.

Will she be entitled to any of it under the law and if so, how much? Or does this just depend on a company's policies?

Leon A., Lorain, OH

PENSION PROTECTION FOR SURVIVORS:

--*Defined benefit and money purchase plans are required to provide the pre-retirement and the post-retirement survivor annuities automattically to married employees, unless a specifie d election to waive survivor coverage is made by both the employee and the spouse.*
--*Choosing a survivor benefit normally reduces the amount paid to the retiree since the pension is calculated on the basis of the joint life expectancy of the participant and the spouse.*
--*ERISA requires that the amount paid to the spouse of the deceased person be at least one-half the amount paid to the retiree, if a joint and survivor option is selected.*

DEAR LEON A: If your plan provides retirement benefits in the form of an annuity, it must also provide one for your surviving spouse in the event of your death after receiving benefits.

this provision is called the joint and survivor annuity. Your survivor will automatically be provided for unless you state in writing that you do not want this to happen. The joint and survivor annuity is a way for you to receive retirement benefits and to have benefits paid to your spouse when you die.

The survivor annuity paid to your spouse myst be at least one-half of the amount that is payable to you under this joint and survivor annuity while you are both living.

Additionally, there may be other provisions in your plan concerning the joint and survivor annuity. You can check through the summary area of your plan. This should be clearly described there. You may also want to discuss this with the benefits manager of your company for clarification.

Changes have been made in the pension law to increase this type of pension protection for the surviving spouses of presently vested employees, as well as for former employees.

You may also want to check this out for clarification with the U.S. Department of Labor to be sure that your company's plan is in compliance.

6. What Are The Benefits For Federal Employees?

DEAR MR. ANSWERMAN: I began working for Federal Civil Service before 1984. Could you please explain how my pension plan will differ from those Federal employees who started working after 1984?

John S., Lawton, OK

FEDERAL EMPLOYEE RETIREMENT COVERAGE PLANS:

--*Civil Service Retirement System (CSRS) is a pre-1984 plan that does not include Social Security coverage.*
--*Federal Employees Retirement System (FERS) is a post-1983 plan that automatically covers employees by Social Security and Medicare.*
--*Thrift Savings Plan (TSP) may be elected by CSRS and FERS participants. The Federal government matches some of the contributions made by FERS participants.*
--*CSRS participants may elect to switch to FERS.*
--*Group health and life insurance plans are available to all Federal employees.*

DEAR JOHN S: Federal civilian employees that were hired before 1984 were not covered by Social Security. The plan that covered them was called the Civil Service Retirement System (CSRS).

Under this plan, a worker aged 55 or over with 30 years of service is eligible for a pension of about 56 percent of the average pay in the highest-paid three years of service.

A worker aged 60 or over with 20 years of Federal service is eligible for about 36 percent of pay. Disability benefits, survivor, and benefits to dependent children are part of CSRS. Benefits are based on the Consumer Price Index and are taxable.

Employees hired after 1983 became part of the Federal Employees Retirement System (FERS). They pay into the Medicare part of the Social Security system and are covered by Social Security retirement benefits.

Under FERS, an employee aged 62 or over with 30 years of service is eligible for a pension of 33 percent of average pay in the highest three years, plus Social Security.

FERS also provides disability and survivor benefits that coordinate with these benefits that are payable under Social Security. These pension benefits are taxable also.

TPS, the thrift savings plan offers an extra method of planning for retirement. A 30 year old Federal employee who starts investing 5 percent of his or her pay in 1991, could have an account of $400,000 by the age of 65.

7. Who Is Entitled To Railroad Retirement Benefits?

DEAR MR. ANSWERMAN: I worked for the railroads for 12 years, but they were not consecutive years. I was also in the army between the times I worked for the railroads.

Could you tell me whether or not I am eligible for benefits and what could I expect in the way of monthly checks?

Jessie S., Erie, PA

FOR MORE INFORMATION:

--For Railroad Retirement board offices look in the blue pages under U.S. Government, Railroad Retirement District Field Office. Many are located in branches of the Post Offices.
--Or write to U.S. Railroad Retirement Board, Chicago, IL 60611
--For Veterans' Benefits contact the VA office nearest you. Check the next few pages for the closest office. Look for the letters VAO.
--Or write to the U.S. Government Printing Office, Washington, DC 20402 and order "Federal Benefits for Veterans and Dependents," Item No. IS-1. Enclose $2.25.

DEAR JESSIE S: I believe you are entitled to benefits, because the Railroad Retirement system is a federally legislated program that provides retirement, disability and survivor annuities to workers whose employment was connected with the railroad industry for at least ten years.

Contact both the Railroad Retirement Board in your area and the nearest Veterans Administration Office. You did not give me very much information about your military service and I don't know what you might be eligible to collect as a Veteran. But, by all means, do contact them to review your case.

Your service with the railroads does not have to be consecutive to be counted and in some cases military service is also counted.

You can start receiving annuities at the age of 62. If you had 30 or more years of service you could start your benefits at the age of 60. In most cases benefits are reduced for early retirement.

If you become disabled after leaving the service, you could be eligible for a retirement pension form the Veterans' Administration (VA). The amount of the pension depends on your age, the severity of your disability, income and the number of dependents you have.

Coverage for your spouse depends on your age, your date of retirement and the years of service as a railroad employee. You are eligible for disability payments at any age if you become permanently disabled. You will have a complicated case, so you should contact both offices as soon as possible.

The following abbreviations are used below:

VAO – VA Office; MC – Medical Center; D – Domiciliary; RO – Regional Office; IC – Insurance Center

ALABAMA

Montgomery (RO) 36104
474 South Court St.

Birmingham (MC) 35233
700 South 19th St.

Montgomery (MC) 36193
215 Perry Hill Rd.

Tuscaloosa (MC) 35404
3401 Loop Rd.

Tuskegee (MC) 36083

ALASKA

Anchorage (RO) 99501
235 E. 8th Ave.

ARIZONA

Phoenix (RO) 85012
3225 North Central Ave.

Phoenix (MC&D) 85012
Seventh St. and Indian
School Rd.

Prescott (MC) 86301

Tucson (MC) 85723

ARKANSAS

Little Rock (RO) 72114
Building 65
Fort Roots
Mailing: P. O. Box 1280
North Little Rock 72215

Fayetteville (MC) 72701

Little Rock (MC)
72205–5484
4300 West Seventh St.

CALIFORNIA (NORTHERN)

San Francisco (RO) 94105
211 Main St.

CALIFORNIA (NORTHERN) (con.)

Fresno (MC) 93703
2615 East Clinton Ave.

Livermore (MC) 94550
4951 Arroyo Rd.

Martinez (MC) 94553
150 Muir Rd.

Palo Alto (MC) 94304
3801 Miranda Ave.

San Francisco (MC) 94121
4150 Clement St.

CALIFORNIA (SOUTHERN)

Los Angeles (RO) 90024
Federal Bldg.
11000 Wilshire Blvd.

San Diego (RO) 92108
2022 Camino Del Rio
North

Loma Linda (MC) 92357
11201 Benton St.

Long Beach (MC) 90822
5901 East Seventh St.

Los Angeles (MC) 90073
(Brentwood)

Los Angeles (MC&D)
90073
(Wadsworth)

San Diego (MC) 92161
3350 La Jolla Village Dr.

Sepulveda (MC) 91343
16111 Plummer St.

COLORADO

Denver (RO) 80225
44 Union Blvd.
P. O. Box 25126

COLORADO (con.)

Denver (MC) 80220
1055 Clermont St.

Fort Lyon (MC) 81038

Grand Junction (MC)
81501

CONNECTICUT

Hartford (RO) 06103
450 Main St.

Newington (MC) 06111
555 Willard Ave.

West Haven (MC) 06516
950 Campbell Ave.

DELAWARE

Wilmington (RO&MC)
19805
1601 Kirkwood Highway

DISTRICT OF COLUMBIA

Washington (RO) 20421
941 North Capitol St., NE
(Benefits to veterans residing in foreign countries not
specifically listed herein
are under the jurisdiction
of VARO, Washington,
D.C.)

Washington (MC) 20422
50 Irving St., NW
(Medical benefits to veterans residing in foreign
countries not specifically
listed herein are under the
jurisdiction of VAMC,
Washington, D.C.)

FLORIDA

St. Petersburg (RO) 33731
P. O. Box 1437
144 First Ave., South

Bay Pines (MC&D) 33504

Gainesville (MC) 32602
1601 S.W. Archer Rd.

FLORIDA (con.)

Jacksonville (VAO) 32206
1833 Boulevard, Rm. 3105

Lake City (MC) 32055

Miami (MC) 33125
1201 Northwest 16th St.

Miami (VAO) 33130
Federal Bldg.
Room 120
51 Southwest First Ave.

Pensacola (VAO) 32503
312 Kenmore Rd., Rm.
1G250

Tampa (MC) 33612
13000 Bruce B. Downs
Blvd.

GEORGIA

Atlanta (RO) 30365
730 Peachtree St., NE

Atlanta (MC) 30033
1670 Clairmont Road

Augusta (MC) 30910
2460 Wrightsboro Rd.

Dublin (MC&D) 31021

HAWAII

(Including American Sa-
moa, Wake, Midway and
the Trust Territory of the
Pacific Islands)
Honolulu (RO) 96813
P. O. Box 50188, 96850
PJKK Federal Bldg.
300 Ala Moana Blvd.

IDAHO

Boise (RO) 83724
Federal Bldg. and
U.S. Courthouse
550 West Fort St., Box 044

Boise (MC) 83702
500 W. Fort St.

ILLINOIS

Chicago (RO) 60680
P. O. Box 8136
536 South Clark St.

ILLINOIS (con.)

Chicago (MC) 60611
(Lakeside)

Chicago (MC) 60680
820 South Damen Ave.
(West Side)

Danville (MC) 61832

Hines (MC) 60141

Marion (MC) 62959
2401 W. Main St.

North Chicago (MC) 60064
3001 Greenbay Rd.

INDIANA

Indianpolis (RO) 46204
575 North Pennsylvania
St.

Fort Wayne (MC) 46805
2121 Lake Ave.

Indianapolis (MC) 46204
1481 West 10th St.

Marion (MC) 46952

IOWA

Des Moines (RO) 50309
210 Walnut St.

Des Moines (MC) 50310
30th and Euclid Ave.

Iowa City (MC) 52240
Highway 6 West

Knoxville (MC) 50138

KANSAS

Wichita (RO&MC) 67218
5500 East Kellogg

Leavenworth (MC&D)
66048

Topeka (MC) 66622
2200 Gage Blvd.

KENTUCKY

Louisville (RO) 40202
600 Martin Luther King, Jr.
Pl.

Lexington (MC&D) 40511

Louisville (MC) 40202
800 Zorn Avenue

LOUISIANA

New Orleans (RO) 70113
701 Loyola Ave.

Alexandria (MC) 71301

New Orleans (MC) 70146
1601 Perdido St.

Shreveport (MC&VAO)
71130
510 East Stoner Ave.

MAINE

Togus (RO&MC) 04330

Portland (VAO) 04101
236 Oxford St.

MARYLAND

Baltimore (RO) 21201
Federal Bldg.
31 Hopkins Plaza

Baltimore (MC) 21218
3900 Loch Raven Blvd.

Fort Howard (MC) 21052

Perry Point (MC) 21902

MASSACHUSETTS

Boston (RO) 02203
John F. Kennedy Bldg.
Government Center

Bedford (MC) 01730
200 Spring Rd.

Boston (MC) 02130
150 South Huntington Ave.

Brockton (MC) 02401

Northampton (MC) 01060

Springfield (VAO) 01103
1200 Main St.

**MASSACHUSETTS
(con.)**

West Roxbury (MC) 02132
1400 Veterans of Foreign
Wars Parkway

MEXICO

(Benefits to veterans residing in Mexico are under jurisdiction of VARO, Hous-
ton, Texas)

MICHIGAN

Detroit (RO) 48226
Patrick V. McNamara
Federal Bldg.
477 Michigan Ave.

Allen Park (MC) 48101

Ann Arbor (MC) 48105
2215 Fuller Rd.

Battle Creek (MC) 49016

Iron Mountain (MC) 49801

Saginaw (MC) 48602
1500 Weiss St.

MINNESOTA

St. Paul (RO&IC) 56111
Federal Bldg.,
Fort Snelling

Minneapolis (MC) 55417
One Veterans Dr.

St. Cloud (MC) 56301

MISSISSIPPI

Jackson (RO) 39269
100 W. Capitol St.

Jackson (MC&D) 39216
1500 East Woodrow
Wilson Dr.

Biloxi (MC&D) 39531
400 Veterans Dr.

MISSOURI

St. Louis (RO) 6310339
Federal Bldg.
1520 Market Street

MISSOURI (con.)

Columbia (MC) 65201
800 Hospital Dr.

Kansas City (MC) 64128
4801 Linwood Blvd.

Kansas City (VAO) 64106
Federal Bldg.
601 East 12th St.

Poplar Bluff (MC) 63901

St. Louis (MC) 63125

MONTANA

Fort Harrison (RO&MC)
59636

Miles City (MC) 59301

NEBRASKA

Lincoln (RO) 68516
5631 S. 48th St.

Grand Island (MC) 68801

Lincoln (MC) 68510
600 South 70th St.

Omaha (MC) 68105
4101 Woolworth Ave.

NEVADA

Reno (RO) 89520
1201 Terminal Way

Reno (MC) 89520
1000 Locust St.

NEW HAMPSHIRE

Manchester (RO) 03101
Norris Cotton Federal
Bldg.
275 Chestnut St.

Manchester (MC) 03104
718 Smyth Rd.

NEW JERSEY

Newark (RO) 07102
20 Washington Place

East Orange (MC) 07019
Tremont and S. Center St.

NEW JERSEY (con.)

Lyons (MC) 07939
Knollcroft Rd.

NEW MEXICO

Albuquerque (RO) 87102
Dennis Chavez Federal
Bldg.
U.S. Courthouse
500 Gold Ave., SW

Albuquerque (MC) 87108
2100 Ridgecrest Dr., SE

NEW YORK(EAST)

New York (RO) 10001
252 Seventh Ave., at
24th St.

Albany (MC) 12208

Albany (VAO) 12207
Leo W. O'Brien Fed. Bldg.
Clinton Ave. and N. Pearl
St.

Bronx (MC) 10468
130 West Kingsbridge Rd.

Brooklyn (MC) 11209
800 Poly Place

Castle Point (MC) 12511

Montrose (MC) 10548

New York (MC) 10010
First Ave. at East 24th St.

Northport (MC) 11768

NEW YORK (WEST)

Buffalo (RO) 14202
Federal Building
111 West Huron St.

Batavia (MC) 14020

Bath (MC) 14810

Buffalo (MC) 14215
3495 Bailey Ave.

**NEW YORK (WEST)
(con.)**

Canandaigua (MC) 14424

Rochester (VAO) 14614
Federal Bldg. and
Courthouse
100 State St.

Syracuse (VAO) 13202
344 W. Genesee St.

Syracuse (MC) 13210
Irving Ave. and University
Pl.

NORTH CAROLINA

Winston–Salem (RO)
27155
Federal Bldg.
251 North Main St.

Asheville (MC) 28805
1100 Tunnel Rd.

Durham (MC) 27705
508 Fulton St.

Fayetteville (MC) 28301
2300 Ramsey St.

Salisbury (MC) 28144
1601 Brenner Ave.

NORTH DAKOTA

Fargo (RO&MC) 58102
655 First Ave. North

Fargo (MC) 58102
2101 Elm St.

OHIO

Cleveland (RO) 44199
Anthony J. Celebrezze
Federal Bldg.
1240 East Ninth St.

Chillicothe (MC) 45601

Cincinnati (MC) 45220
3200 Vine St.

Cincinnati (VAO) 45202
The Society, Suite 210
36 East 7th St.

**OHIO
(con.)**

Cleveland (MC) 44106
10701 East Boulevard

Columbus (VAO) 43215
Federal Bldg., Room 309
200 North High St.

Dayton (MC&D) 45428

OKLAHOMA

Muskogee (RO) 74401
Federal Bldg.
125 South Main St.

Muskogee (MC) 74401

Oklahoma City (MC)
73014
921 Northeast 13th St.

Oklahoma City (VAO)
73102
Federal Bldg.
200 Northwest Fourth St.

OREGON

Portland (RO) 97204
Federal Bldg.
1220 Southwest Third Ave.

Portland (MC) 97207
3710 Southwest
U.S. Veterans Hospital
Road

Roseburg (MC) 97470

White City (D) 97501

PENNSYLVANIA (EAST)

Philadelphia (RO&IC)
19101
P.O. Box 8079
5000 Wissahickon Ave.

Coatsville (MC) 19320

Lebanon (MC) 17042
1700 S. Lincoln Ave.

Philadelphia (MC) 19104
Univ. and Woodland Aves.

**PENNSYLVANIA (EAST)
(con.)**

Wilkes–Barre (VAO) 18701
19–17 North Main St.

Wilkes–Barre (MC) 18711
1111 East End Blvd.

PENNSYLVANIA (WEST)

Pittsburgh (RO) 15222
1000 Liberty Ave.

Altoona (MC) 16602
2907 Pleasant Valley Blvd.

Butler (MC) 16001

Erie (MC) 16504
135 East 38th St.

Pittsburgh (MC) 15206
Highland Dr.

Pittsburgh (MC) 15240
University Drive C

PHILIPPINES

Manila (RO) 96528
1131 Roxas Blvd.
APO San Francisco

**PUERTO RICO,
COMMONWEALTH OF**
(including the Virgin Is-
lands)

San Juan (RO) 00918
Federico Degetau Fed.
Bldg. and Courthouse
Carlos E. Chardon Ave.
Gregg St.
Hato Rey

San Juan (MC) 00921
Barrio Monacillos
Rio Piedras

Providence (RO) 02903
380 Westminster Mall

RHODE ISLAND

Providence (RO) 02903
380 Westminster Mall

Providence (MC) 02908
Davis Park

SOUTH CAROLINA

Columbia (RO) 29201
1801 Assembly St.

Charleston (MC) 29403
109 Bee St.

Columbia (MC) 29201

SOUTH DAKOTA

Sioux Falls (RO&MC)
57117
P. O. Box 5046
2501 W. 22nd St.

Fort Meade (MC) 57741

Hot Springs (MC&D)
57747

TENNESSEE

Nashville (RO) 37203
110 Ninth Ave., South

Memphis (MC) 38104
1030 Jefferson Ave.

Mountain Home (MC&D)
37601

Murfreesboro (MC) 37130
3400 Lebanon Rd.

Nashville (MC) 37203
1310 24th Ave., South

TEXAS (NORTHERN)

Waco (RO) 76799
1400 North Valley Mills
Drive

Amarillo (MC) 79106
6010 Amarillo Blvd., W.

Big Spring (MC) 79720
2400 S. Gregg St.

Bonham (MC&D) 75418
9th & Lipscomb

Dallas (VAO) 75242
U.S. Courthouse and
Federal Bldg.
1100 Commerce St.

TEXAS (NORTHERN)
(con.)

Dallas (MC) 75216
4500 South Lancaster Rd.

Fort Worth (VAO) 76102
819 Taylor St.

Lubbock (VAO) 79410
U.S. Courthouse and
Federal Bldg.
1205 Texas Ave.

Marlin (MC) 76661
1016 Ward St.

Temple (MC&D) 76501
1901 S. 1st St.

Waco (MC) 76711
4800 Memorial Drive

TEXAS (SOUTHERN)

Houston (RO) 77054
2515 Murworth Dr.

Houston (MC) 77211
2002 Holcombe Blvd.

Kerrville (MC) 78028

San Antonio (VAO)
78229–2041
3601 Bluemel Rd.

San Antonio (MC) 78284
7400 Merton Minter Blvd.

UTAH

Salt Lake City (RO) 84147
Federal Bldg.
125 South State St.

Salt Lake City (MC) 84148
500 Foothill Blvd.

VERMONT

White River Junction
(RO&MC) 05009

VIRGINIA

Roanoke (RO) 24011
210 Franklin Rd., SW

Hampton (MC&D) 23667
100 Emancipation Rd.

VIRGINIA
(con.)

Richmond (MC) 23249
1201 Broad Rock Rd.

Salem (MC) 24153
1970 Blvd. & Roanoke

WASHINGTON

Seattle (RO) 98174
Federal Bldg.
915 Second Ave.

Tacoma (MC) 98493
American Lake

Seattle (MC) 98108
1660 South Columbian
Way

Spokane (MC) 99208
North 4815 Assembly St.

Walla Walla (MC) 99362
77 Wainwright Drive

WEST VIRGINIA

Huntington (RO) 25701
640 Fourth Ave.

WEST VIRGINIA
(con.)

Beckley (MC) 25801
200 Veterans Ave.

Clarksburg (MC) 26301

Huntington (MC) 25704
1540 Spring Valley Dr.

Martinsburg (MC&D)
25401

WISCONSIN

Milwaukee (RO) 53295
5000 West National Ave.
Bldg. 6

Madison (MC) 53705
2500 Overlook Terrace

Tomah (MC) 54660

Milwaukee (MC&D) 53295
5000 West National Ave.

WYOMING

Cheyenne (RO&MC)
82001
2360 East Pershing Blvd.

Sheridan (MC) 82801

8. Are There Any Retirement Benefits In Life Insurance?

DEAR MR. ANSWERMAN: My life insurance agent has been after me to buy a policy which he claims will provide me with good retirement income.

He says I should buy a policy which builds cash value rather than a cheaper kind that just pays a death benefit. This way, he maintains, I can have cash when I need it. Could you tell me more about life insurance as a retirement investment?

Richard R., Albany, NY

TYPES OF LIFE INSURANCE:

--TERM builds no cash value. The holder must die before any money can be paid out. Many employers offer group term policies as a benefit. Premiums are usually quite low.
--WHOLE (ORDINARY, STRAIGHT LIFE) have higher premiums that remain fixed. Payments build cash value that can be collected to supplement retirement income.
--VARIABLE policies build cash value that is tied directly to certain investments of the insurance company.
--UNIVERSAL policies allow the policy holder to change the amount of coverage by paying a smaller or larger than normal premium.

DEAR RICHARD R: Whole life policies, which is what I think your insurance agent may be trying to convince you to buy, are often described as savings vehicles, but protection is their main purpose.

If you purchase a whole life insurance policy early in your life, it can build some cash value that could be used to supplement retirement income.

Those who bought whole life insurance 20 or 30 years ago, should find out the type of insurance they have, its current and paid-up value, and its loan and conversion options. It is a good idea to also check to that the beneficiary designations are up-to-date and that someone is also named as the second beneficiary, in case the first one dies before the policy holder does.

Policy holders and their families need to know what policies they have, their values, and where they are located. It's best not to keep insurance policies in a safe deposit box, since access can be difficult at the time of death.

It is also a good idea to review the fine print of any policies you might have or are thinking of buying.

Those who are already retired will probably need less life insurance coverage, especially if there are no dependent children to support and educate. Most providers want to feel that there will be enough funds for a surviving spouse to handle immediate burial expenses. If there is a lot of cash in a policy, it probably can earn more interest in some other type of investment than in insurance.

9. What Are The Advantages Of Buying An Annuity?

DEAR MR. ANSWERMAN: Recently, I have been considering investing my lump sum pension into an annuity. But there are so many different kinds of annuities that I am confused.

Could you explain the differences between a deferred annuity, a single premium deferred annuity, an intermediate pay annuity, and a variable annuity?

Susan B., Rockford, IL

TYPES OF ANNUITIES:

--DEFERRED annuities require the policyholder to make premium payments each year.
--SINGLE PREMIUM deferred annuities require a lump sum payment.
--INTERMEDIATE PAY annuities also require a lump sum payment. It is designed for those of retirement age. Fixed monthly payments begin right away.
--VARIABLE annuities place the premiums into an account that fluctuates as economic conditions change. The return is not fixed as other types are.

DEAR SUSAN B: Annuities are contracts between life insurance companies and individuals. The buyer of the annuity pays a given sum and receives, in return, a guaranteed fixed income for a specified period of time or for life. As a rule, the older you are when you purchase and annuity, the higher your payments to purchase an annuity will be.

If I understand your situation correctly, I believe you are either already retired or just about to. I would therefore suggest an "intermediate pay annuity," preferably one that pays for life and has good death benefit options for your survivors.

Annuities have some definite advantages:

* They free you from the responsibility of managing money.
* You will not be tempted to use the lump sum for other purposes and deplete your assets.
* They guarantee a steady income for life.
* You are able to defer Federal income tax because the annuity income isn't taxed during working years, but is taxable in part after retirement.

It is best not to sink all your assets into annuities since monthly fixed payments do not keep pace with inflation.

Do shop around and compare the yields and payment options offered by different insurance companies and other financial institutions. Don't forget to ask if you will be charged with administration fees, sales commissions, and what they are. Also, read the fine print.

10. What Are Some Good Investing Strategies?

DEAR MR. ANSWERMAN: I've been seeing in the newspapers and on TV how elderly people who have been milked out of their retirement nest eggs by unscrupulous investment counselors.

How can someone protect themselves against junk bond frauds and other investment gimmicks to protect investment money?

Francis M., Memphis, TN

INVESTMENT STRATEGIES:

—SAFETY VS. RISK

—DIVERSITY

—INCOME

—LIQUIDITY

—GROWTH

—TAXABILITY

DEAR FRANCIS M: Memorize the six important factors to consider when making investments for your retirement. I have listed them under your letter.

Safety vs. Risk — With safer investments you usually get a lower rate of return. If you want a higher rate, you will be taking some risks. You should never accept risks that you feel uncomfortable about. The older you are the less you can afford to lose any money.

Diversity — Don't put all your eggs in one basket. A variety of investments protect you in case one of them fails. Remember that nothing is fail-proof.

Income — How much income will you need from your investments for living expenses? Do you need it for regular income or can you set aside money to re-invest for the long term? Don't risk what you need to support yourself with during retirement.

Liquidity — Three to six months of living expenses need to be kept liquid to meet normal living and unexpected expenses. Investments like real estate are not easily made liquid, while others impose penalties if you cash them in prematurely.

Growth — Typically the more growth there is, the higher the risk you will assume. You need to rate security higher than growth during retirement years.

Taxability — The rate the investment is taxed is an important factor. Some investments are free from Federal taxes, but not from State and Local taxes, or vice versa.

V: IRAs AND OTHER INVESTMENTS

1. How Much Should I Set Aside In Savings?

DEAR MR. ANSWERMAN: While I'm still about ten years away from retiring, I would like to know how much of my retirement program I should be devoting to savings.

Considering all the trouble with the banks today, how reliable are they? I want to feel secure about my savings plans for the next ten years, because this is my last chance to prepare for my retirement.

Harold B., Roanoke, VA

TYPES OF ACCOUNTS THAT ARE INSURED BY THE FEDERAL DEPOSIT INSURANCE CORPORATION (FDIC):

--Savings accounts in federally insured banks
--Savings accounts in federally insured savings and loan institutions
--Savings accounts in federally insured credit unions
--Up to $100,000 in each of these types of accounts
--Certificates of deposit in financial institutions federally insured

DEAR HAROLD B: The safest savings are the ones that are insured by the FDIC. Before you open an account in a bank, savings and loan institution, or credit union be sure it is federally insured. And verify it from the written documents the institution gives you.

Passbook Savings Accounts are the safest savings, but they earn interest at a rate that barely keeps pace with inflation.

To get the best yield, select an account that compounds interest from the day of deposit to the day of withdrawal. You will, of course, have to pay taxes on the interest earned.

These accounts do offer you liquidity in a case of emergency and they are safe, but do consider the inflation factor. If you examine the chart on the next page, you can see what happens when you begin to dip into your savings.

If you can build up enough of a cash reserve to live comfortably on the interest only from your lifetime savings, you will be able to maintain the principle.

If you find it necessary to make regular withdrawals from your savings to help finance your retirement, then do it cautiously. If you take less each month, you may still be able to maintain a good balance.

While you are still working, a good rule of thumb for savings is between 3 and 10 percent of your current income.

Dipping Into Your Nest Egg

Starting with a lump sum of . . .	. . . you can withdraw this much each month for the stated number of years, reducing the nest egg to zero					. . . OR, you can withdraw this much each month and always have the original nest egg intact.
	10 yrs.	15 yrs.	20 yrs.	25 yrs.	30 yrs.	
$ 10,000	$ 107	$ 81	$ 68	$ 61	$ 56	$ 46
15,000	161	121	102	91	84	69
20,000	215	162	136	121	112	92
25,000	269	202	170	152	140	115
30,000	322	243	204	182	168	138
40,000	430	323	272	243	224	184
50,000	537	404	340	304	281	230
60,000	645	485	408	364	337	276
80,000	859	647	544	486	449	368
100,000	1,074	808	680	607	561	460

(Based on an interest rate of 5.5% per year, compounded quarterly).

2. What Are Some Other Risk-Free Alternatives?

DEAR MR. ANSWERMAN: I am looking for some risk-free alternatives to savings accounts, because the interest they pay is so small these days.

I need to have my savings earn as much interest as possible to help me supplement my retirement. But I am concerned about not losing my savings. I don't want to end up like a lot of older people I hear about who put their money into bad investments and ended up losing their nest eggs.

Can you explain the differences between CDs and Money Market Funds? Which ones are the safest and which ones will give me the best interest rates?

Sheryl A., Sunnyvale, CA

CERTIFICATES OF DEPOSIT (CDs):

—*Available from financial institutions in varying denominations*
—*Pays higher interest than savings accounts*
—*Interest is subject to taxation*
—*Are federally insured*

MONEY MARKET FUNDS:

—*Available from financial institutions in varying denominations*
—*Pay as high-interest as short-term instruments.*
—*Usually no sales charge.*
—*Interest rates change daily.*
—*Not federally insured.*
—*Interest is subject to taxation.*

DEAR SHERYL A: Certificates of deposit are a good investment. They are fully insured and can return a good yield. The philosophy behind them is that the larger your deposit and the longer the term of the CD, the higher interest you will be paid. You can often double your investments within 8 to 10 years.

Be sure to compare maturities and interest rates in banks and S&Ls just in case you need to cash one in before maturity. There are usually penalties involved in early withdrawal. You will also have to pay taxes on the interest they earn.

Money Market Funds are not federally insured, but are relatively safe. They were established in the early 1970s and allow small investors to pool their assets to get high-quality, high-interest, short-term instruments, like U.S. Government Securities and large CDs. Often you can invest as little as $500 or $1000 and can withdraw your money at any time without a penalty.

The interest rates with Money Market Funds fluctuate with inflation. Many of these type of accounts allow you to write checks against your account. Because they fluctuate and are subject to taxes, you should use these as short-term investments and ones that you need to monitor frequently.

These can be purchased through banks and other financial institutions.

3. What Are The Advantages Of IRAs And Keoughs?

DEAR MR. ANSWERMAN: Even though I contribute to a company pension plan, I have been told that I can still set aside a considerable amount of money to a tax-free personal retirement fund called an IRA.

I would appreciate it if you could give me some basic information about IRAs. How do they differ from Keoughs?

William M., Fairfax, VT

WITHDRAWAL RULES FOR IRAs KEOUGHs:

—*Penalties apply for withdrawals before the age of 59 1/2 years.*

—*The penalty for early withdrawal is 10 percent.*

—*Penalties do not apply if you become totally disabled.*

—*Penalties do not apply if you die.*

—*Penalties do not apply if you withdraw in the form of a lifetime annuity.*

—*You must start withdrawing funds by the year after you reach age 70 1/2.*

TAX INFORMATION ON IRSs AND KEOUGHs:

—*Contact your local IRS office and ask them to send you Publication 590, "Tax Information on Individual Retirement Arrangements."*

DEAR WILLIAM M: The Tax Reform Act of 1986, unfortunately, nullified tax deferrals for IRA contributions of workers already covered by employer retirement plans.

There is an exception for those with an adjusted gross income that is below certain amounts. It is $25,000 for a single person and $40,000 for joint filers. Contributions are then in part tax-deferred up to $35,000 for single and $50,000 for joint filers. Those who are not allowed a deferral can still make non-deductible contributions up the annual allowable maximum, which is $2000 for each individual.

Self-employed people, part or full time, may set up a Keough account. These plans allow you to put money away for retirement on your own and defer paying tax on that money and the accrued interest until you retire.

IRAs and Keoughs are both administered by financial institutions, stockbrokers, and life insurance companies. Some plans have administrative costs and some yield higher interest rates than others.

Keough plans now have equal footing with corporate pension plans. Self-employed persons may take a tax deduction for annual contributions to the plan, limited to the lesser amount of $30,000 or 25 percent of earned income. Keough plans must also make tax-deductible contributions for the benefit of any employees.

With IRA plans the employer does not have to make contributions to employees, but the allowable deduction is much lower at $2000 for each individual.

4. How Good Are Bonds For Retirement?

DEAR MR. ANSWERMAN: My accountant has suggested that I look at the bond market to fund my retirement program. The only problem is that the information he has given me doesn't answer all my questions and concerns.

What is the difference, for instance, between U.S. Government bonds, corporate bonds, and municipal bonds?

I read an article about zero coupon bonds and wonder what they are. Can you tell me about these and any others I may not have heard about?

Kenneth H., Casper, WY

TYPES OF BONDS:

- *--U.S. Government (not U.S. Savings Bonds) include Treasury notes, short-term Treasury bills, and long term bonds.*
- *--Corporate bonds are issued by companies with ratings from a high of AAA to a low of C.*
- *--Municipal bonds are issued by cities and carry the same ratings as corporate bonds.*
- *--Zero Coupon Bonds are popular for long-term investments. It can be issued by a corporation or and agency of the federal, state, or local government. They are sold at below face value.*
- *--U.S. Savings Bonds are safe and convenient and available in small denominations.*

DEAR KENNETH H: The general characteristics of bonds is that they are sold in stated dollar values and pay a fixed interest rate. They can be issued by the federal government, by a corporation, a municipality, or an agency of the government.

They are designed as a means of raising funds, usually for specific purposes. They can be redeemed at full value when they mature, usually from 10 to 25 years or more. If you cash them in early, however, you may have to sell them at a loss.

Bonds are a conservative investment that can offer you a low risk, as well as assured income. They are not good for quick profit.

Municipal bonds are relatively safe. Be sure to check their ratings with Standard and Poors and Moodys before you purchase them. A stockbroker or information in a library will be able to give you specific ratings for a bond option. The return is usually only 5 to 7 percent, but it is offset by a tax exemption.

Zero Coupon Bonds is that growth is assured since the interest is added on at the end, so that is will be worth more than the price you paid for it. Of course, it is not possible to know for sure what the future value of the bond will be at maturity.

U.S. Savings bonds are the safest. You can cash them in at any time, but you will not get their full value until maturity.

Some other government bonds to investigate are EE and HH bonds. The EE bonds must be held for 5 years, and the HH bonds pay dividends twice a year.

5. Should I Invest
   In The Stock Market?

DEAR MR. ANSWERMAN: Two friends of mine are always having the same argument about the stock market. My friend Al says that he always does well in the stock market, no matter if it goes up or down. But Joe, who argues with Al, says that he prefers to invest his money in collectibles, rather than in stocks or mutual funds.

What is your opinion about these two different kinds of investments?

Robert L., Greenville, SC

SOME DEFINITIONS:

—*Common stocks represent a part ownership in a company.*

—*Preferred shares in a company have a stated income and you receive a fixed return.*

—*Mutual funds pool assets with those of other small investors to offer balance and diversification of holdings. They are professionally managed.*

—*Collectibles are items such as gold, silver, art, and antiques that have value and a potential for growth.*

DEAR ROBERT L: Stocks, mutual funds, and collectibles all carry some risk, since making money with them depends a lot on the market demand. All of these forms of investment should be viewed as long-term ones.

Often the market is excellent for a particular type of investment and at other times, especially during recessionary periods, gains can be slow, static, or non-existent. And there is always a chance for losses.

That is why I like to caution people to know what they are doing. Do some research on companies you are considering buying stock from. The same holds true about mutual funds. Some stocks have an excellent track record and so do some mutual funds, but the past does not always tell you what will happen tomorrow.

Deal with a reputable stockbroker and firm when buying and selling stocks. You will be paying them commissions.

Preferred shares are usually more secure, since they are paid before common shares. Mutual funds are good for smaller investors since they pool money and diversify the investments. Fees are also charged. Some mutual funds specialize in tax free income sources, which can be beneficial for retirement income. Find out if the mutual fund has a "load" or "no-load" feature. Load funds charge initially and annually as well. No-load funds charge for service later, but not initially.

To invest in collectibles, you should know a lot about the item. Remember they can be stolen and should be insured.

6. Where Should I Live In Retirement?

DEAR MR. ANSWERMAN: I am planning to relocate for my retirement to a warmer climate.

The house I now own is a large one. My children are all grown up and gone. There doesn't seem to be much point in trying to hold on the house, since it would cost a lot to keep up.

Could you give me some general guidelines on how to approach this problem of where to live in retirement?

Martha V., Gary, IN

ONCE-IN-A-LIFETIME EXCLUSION:

—*If you or your spouse is 55 or older, you are entitled to a once-in-a-lifetime exclusion from federal income tax of up to $125,000 profit on the sale of your home.*

__*Since this exclusion is allowed only once to a homeowner, it should be considered very carefully in making present and future home buying plans. Once you take it, you cannot take it again.*

DEAR MARTHA V: If you have owned your house for a long time, it has in all likelihood appreciated in value and kept pace with inflation, probably better than most other investments.

If you hold on to your home, you will still protect the equity, the amount the house is worth minus what you may owe in a mortgage, and you can still sell it later on.

You might want to consider the condition of the real estate market at the time you decide to sell. If prices in real estate are up, it is usually a good time to sell. But there are periods when real estate prices are down, and you might do better to wait several years if that is the case.

Other things to consider, as you said in your letter, are the costs of upkeep and the size of the house. You could consider renting out the house at first when you relocate, until you are sure about the move you plan to make to a warmer climate.

Other considerations are taxes and utility costs and the housing costs in your new location. Generally, the cost of housing should represent no more than one-third of your net income.

Total how much it costs you each month to live in your present house. Compare these with the costs of renting, owning a smaller house or a condominium, and the cost of housing in the area you are planning to move to.

Spend some time in the other location to be sure you are comfortable about the climate and location.

7. Is Real Estate Still A Good Investment?

DEAR MR. ANSWERMAN: In the past real estate investments were considered good buys for retirees.

How risky is real estate in today's market?

Ruth E., Sioux Falls, SD

CONSIDERATIONS WHEN INVESTING IN REAL ESTATE:

--What are the current market conditions?

--How long does it takes to sell real estate property in my area?

--Have prices remained stable, risen, or fallen in the last six months?

--What will my tax responsibilities be when I own real estate?

--What are the costs of maintaining a property?

--Will there be tenant-management disputes that will eat up my profits?

--What will the upkeep cost?

--What condition is the property in?

--Will there be major renovations needed within the next few years?

--Never buy anything you haven't seen, especially land.

--Has the contract for a purchase in real estate been carefully analyzed by a lawyer?

DEAR RUTH E: As with every major investment, and real estate is always major, "buyer beware."

You must do careful research and analysis. The options that you have when you live in a property that you own are not the same as the ones that you buy as an investment.

By renting out your home after you retire, or by buying rental property, you may have the opportunity to supplement your income, be eligible for certain tax breaks, and have your investment appreciate in value.

However, this also poses some potential risks and you need to approach it with caution. Remember, there is no guarantee your investment will appreciate in value. The real estate has suffered a serious down turn in many parts of the country because of the economy.

As a landlord, you have the responsibility for managing the property or entrusting it to a real estate agent for a fee. Consider this before buying. Costs for upkeep, taxes and utilities are other factors to include when you calculate your profits.

While over the years, real estate has been profitable for many, it can be risky. It can also tie up your money, since this investment has no liquidity. If the market for real estate is down, it can be hard to sell and get your price. You might even suffer a loss if you have to sell at a bad time.

Consider real estate only if you feel very secure about your knowledge and ability to handle the responsibilities involved.

8. What Are Some Of The Home Equity Conversion Plans?

DEAR MR. ANSWERMAN: I have decided to stay in my home when I retire because I own it free and clear.

Is there any way for me to use the equity in my house without losing my house?

Mary Lou P., Norfolk, VA

WHY YOU MIGHT CONSIDER A HOME EQUITY CONVERSION:

--It is your only large asset.
--Property taxes.
--Inflation.
--Home maintenance costs.
--Repairs to the home.
--High medical costs.
--Emergency needs.

REASONS NOT TO CONSIDER A HOME EQUITY CONVERSTION:

--The desire to travel.
--New furniture.
--An expensive car.
--Helping a friend or family member who has some extraordinary financial problem.
--To make some other investment.

DEAR MARY LOU P: With the advent of the innovative home equity conversion loans, retired individuls can now use the equity in their homes as a source of income without having to move or sell their house.

Although there are a number of different types of home equity conversion plans, they all operate on the same principle of providing a source of income for homeowners, while letting them live in their homes.

Some plans invlove the actual sale and transfer of the property to a lending institution. Others do not.

Some provide income for only a specific period of time. Others will guarantee a level of income for life. Other plans involve a lending institution loaning you money on the value of your house. This loan is used to then purchase an annuity that provides the holder with a monthly income.

When you move or die, your home is sold and the proceeds are used to pay off the loan. If there is a remaining balance, it goes to your estate.

This arrangement is not good for everyone. These are complex financial arrangements. There could be serious problems that could come from them, if you do not fully understand them and your obligations under the agreements.

It is critical that you get sound legal and financial advice before you enter into a home equity conversion agreement.

9. How Do I Prepare A Retirement Budget?

DEAR MR. ANSWERMAN: While I am busy preparing my investment program for retirement, I am also concerned about how to set up a retirement budget.

Do you have any advice for an approach to this problem?

Terry S., Baltimore, MD

BUDGET CATEGORIES:

--Housing
--Food
--Clothing
--Personal care
--Transportation
--Health care
--Life insurance
--Retirement contributions
--Other savings
--Contributions
--Entertainment
--Recreation
--Travel
--Household items
--Gifts
--Miscellaneous out-of-pocket expenses

DEAR TERRY S: Begin by calculating your net income, the amount that you and your family receive monthly from all sources, after deductions are made.

Use the worksheet on the next page, "Your Budget Today." Major budget categories are listed under your letter. Be sure to include all of them. Include both your fixed expenses and the ones that vary from month to month. Clothing might be something that you only buy seasonally.

At the end of each month total all expenses under each heading. Add the expense totals together and subtract expenses from total income. Keep all your receipts for budgeting and income tax purposes.

To estimate your retirement budget, again list all your potential sources of income. And again estimate how much you sill spend each month. Use the worksheet on page 73, "Your Retirement Budget" to help make your calculations.

Unfortunately, there is no way to predict the rate of inflation or its effects in the coming years. Social Security benefits continue to rise with the cost of living, but pension benefits probably will not.

Review the chart on page 72, "Projecting Retirement Income for Inflation." This will give you some idea of how to plan your retirement budget needs.

Retired persons living on fixed incomes need to be cautious about using credit cards for major purchases. The added interest rate will make it even harder to stay within your budget than just keeping up with inflation.

Your Budget for Today

Monthly Income Received Now

Wages & Salary _____

Other Income _____

Bank Account Interest _____

Stock & Bond Dividends _____

Annuities _____

Other Investments _____

Total: _____

How Much You Spend Each Month

Housing _____

Food _____

Clothing &
Personal Care _____

Transportation _____

Health Care _____

Life Insurance _____

Savings &
Investments _____

Contributions _____

Other Expenses _____

Total: _____

Total Income _____

Total Expenses _____

Differences,
Plus or Minus _____

71

Projecting Retirement Income for Inflation

Yearly Retirement Expenses
(Monthly Retirement Expenses Multiplied by 12)

Inflation Impact Table
(Compounded at 4% per year)

1	1.0400	16	1.8730
2	1.0816	17	1.9480
3	1.1249	18	2.0260
4	1.1699	19	2.1070
5	1.2167	20	2.1913
6	1.2654	21	2.2790
7	1.3160	22	2.3702
8	1.3686	23	2.4650
9	1.4234	24	2.5636
10	1.4803	25	2.6661
11	1.5395	26	2.7727
12	1.6011	27	2.8836
13	1.6651	28	2.9989
14	1.7317	29	3.1189
15	1.8010	30	3.2437

Housing _____

Food _____

Cotthing &
Personal Care _____

Transportation _____

Health Care _____

Life Insurance _____

Projection for Inflation

Multiply the total from the Yearly Retirement Expenses column by appropriate inflation factor from the Inflation Impact Table. For example, if you are five years form retirement, you'll use Inflation Factor 1.2167 to learn how much you'll actually need that first retirement year. After that, project for five years into retirement and make any other projections you think are necessary.

Your first retirement year:	Five Years after retirement:	Further projections:
_____	_____	_____

Savings &
Investments _____

Contributions _____

Other Expenses _____

Total: ═══════════

Be sure to apply the Inflation Factor only to those items that are subject to inflation.

72

Your Retirement Budget

Estimated Monthly Retirement Income		What You Think You'll Need After Retirement	
Social Security	_____	Housing	_____
Other Government Pension	_____	Food	_____
Company Pension	_____	Clothing & Personal Care	_____
Employment Wages	_____	Transportation	_____
Cash Accounts:		Health Care	_____
Checking	_____	Life Insurance	_____
Savings	_____	Savings & Investments	_____
Life Insurance Annuities	_____		
IRA & Keogh Payments	_____	Contributions	_____
Stock & Bond Dividends	_____	Other Expenses	_____
Other Investments	_____		
Sale of Home or Business	_____	Total:	_____
Total:	_____		

Total Income _____

Total Expenses _____

Difference, Plus or Minus _____

73

10. How Do I Estimate My Net Worth?

DEAR MR. ANSWERMAN: I have a two-part question.

How do I estimate my net worth?

How much will I need in retirement?

Another question that come to mind after I get the answers to these two questions is what happens if my retirement budget doesn't balance?

Daniel D., Eugene, OR

CHECK LIST FOR SOURCES OF INCOME:

--Social Security
--Other retirement income from pensions
--Private company pensions
--Salary/wages from employment
--Cash accounts:
   * Savings
   * Checking
   * CDs
   * Money market funds
--Life insurance annuities
--IRA/Keogh plans
--Stock/Bond dividends
--Corporate securities
--Government securities
--Other investments
   * Real estate
   * Collectibles
   * Mutual funds
--Sale of business
--Sale of home

DEAR DANIEL D: Net worth defines all your assets and debts. Use the worksheet on the next page to help you prepare yours. This information needs to be written down to be of any use to you in planning your retirement and what you will need to be comfortable.

Set up two columns, one for assets and one for liabilities. If the worth of personal property and valuables are hard to determine, make the best estimate that you can, but aim low. It won't help you to overestimate your worth for retirement planning.

In the liabilities column include all current outstanding bills, mortgages remaining on your house, charge account and installment debts, and any other outstanding loans. When you have completed assets and liabilities, subtract your total liabilities from your total assets and that is your net worth.

As far as what you will need for retirement, go back to question 9 in this section, which talks about preparing a retirement budget.

Retirement income should represent between 65 to 75 percent of your pre-retirement income. Your spending patterns and expenses will likely change during retirement. You will also benefit from the help you get from Medicare for medical expenses once you reach 65. There are also many "senior citizen" discounts to help you with transportation, entertainment, and other needs.

Take a look at the chart of page 76, "Average Annual Expenditures, 65+ Household" for budgeting help.

Net Worth

Assets -- What We Own	Bill and Nancy	Your Figures
Cash:		
Checking Account	$ 800	_____
Savings Account	4,500	_____
Investments:		
U.S. Savings Bonds (Current cash-in value)	5,000	_____
Stocks, mutual funds	4,500	_____
Life Insurance:		
Cash value, accumulated dividends	10,000	_____
Company Pension Rights:		
Accrued pension benefit	20,000	_____
Property:		
House (resale value)	50,000	_____
Furniture and appliances	8,000	_____
Collections and jewelry	2,000	_____
Automobile	3,000	_____
Other:		
Loan to brother	1,000	_____
Gross Assets	**$108,800**	_____
Liabilities -- What We Owe		
Current Unpaid Bills	600	_____
Home Mortgage (remaining balance)	9,700	_____
Auto Loan	1,200	_____
Property Taxes	1,100	_____
Hoime Improvement Loan	3,700	_____
Total Liabilities	**$16,300**	_____

Net Worth: Assets of $108,800 minus liabilities of $16,300 equals $92,500.

Average Annual Expenditures
Older (65+) Household

Category	Amount	Percent of Total
Housing	$6,168.00	33%
Transportation	3,092.00	16%
Food	2,912.00	16%
Health Care	2,135.00	11%
Clothing & Personal Care	1,179.00	6%
Contributions	1,091.00	6%
Entertainment, Reading & Education	927.00	5%
Life Insurance/Pensions	740.00	4%
Miscellaneous	439.00	3%
Total:	**$ 18,967.00**	**100%**

Source: Bureau of Labor Statistics, 1989.

VI: MEDICARE, MEDICAID AND NURSING HOMES

1. How Does Medicare Protect My Income?

DEAR MR. ANSWERMAN: At age 65 I understand that I will be eligible for Medicare whether or not I take my Social Security retirement at that time.

I would like to know more about Medicare, especially how effective it will be in protecting my income if I should have an accident or become ill. Can you give me some information and guidelines?

Phyllis A., Huntington, WV

MEDICARE PART A:

—*Hospital Insurance Program*
—*Eligible at age 65*
—*Covers inpatient services*
—*Covers 100 days of care in a skilled nursing facility*
—*Covers home health care*
—*Covers hospice for terminally ill persons*
—*Annual deductible*

MEDICARE PART B:

—*Supplementary Medical Insurance Program*
—*Monthly premiums*
—*Low premiums*
—*Covers outpatient services*
—*Covers physician's fees*
—*Covers physical therapy and other services*
—*Annual deductible*

DEAR PHYLLIS A: Don't underestimate the value of Medicare. This program is essential to older retired persons in these days of skyrocketing medical costs.

Medicare is a two-part federal health insurance program for men and women who are 65 and over, and the severely disabled who are under 65.

When you apply for Social Security, you will receive information about Medicare. But you do not have to be retired to receive Medicare benefits.

If you choose not to retire before reaching the age of 65, you should still apply for Medicare at your local Social Security Office, at least three months before your 65th birthday. Then your coverage will begin as soon as you are eligible.

Medicare, while it gives excellent coverage, does not cover all health care costs. Routine check-ups, non-prescription drugs, eye glasses and exams, routine dental care, hearing tests and most long-term care assistance are some of the services that Medicare does not cover.

Keep a record of all your out-of-pocket medical costs for income tax purposes.

There are also deductibles in both Parts A and B of Medicare coverage, just as in most commercial health insurance plans.

Ask your Social Security office to send you two pamphlets: "A Brief Explanation of Medicare" and "Your Medicare Handbook."

2. Do I Need Any Medical Insurance Besides Medicare?

DEAR MR. ANSWERMAN: My insurance agent has shown me a Medicare supplemental insurance policy. I thought that Medicare would give me all the coverage that I need, but he says it will not and I need the extra coverage.

I would like more information on how necessary these policies are and how to go about judging them. Can you help me?

Scott W., Warwick, RI

FREE MEDICARE PUBLICATIONS:

--Medicare Handbook
--Guide to Health Insurance for People with Medicare (507-X)
--Medicare and Coordinated Care Plans (509-X)
--Medicare Hospice Beneftis (508-X)
--Medicare and Employer Health Plans (586-X)
--Getting A Second Opinion (536-X)
--Medicare Coverage of Kidney Dialysis and Kidney Transplant Services (587-X)
--Medicare Secondary Payer

Ask your Social Security office or write to:
    Medicare Publications
    Health Care Financing Admin.
    6325 Security Boulevard
    Baltimore, MD 21207

MEDIGAP COMPLAINT LINE:
    1-800-638-6833

DEAR SCOTT W: Private health insurance designed to supplement Medicare's benefits by filling in some of Medicare's coverage is called Medigap.

This coverage generally pays for Medicare approved charges not paid by Medicare because of deductibles or coinsurance amounts for which you are liable.

Before buying a Medigap policy, you should compare several from differenct companies, since they have different combinations of benefits.

In 1992 most States are expected to adopt regulations limiting the Medigap insurance market to no more than 10 standard policies. One of the 10 will be a basic policy offering a core package of beneftis. The other 9 will have to include the core package, but will have a different combination of benefits.

If you decide to gct Mcdigap, you will only need one good policy that meets your needs at a price you can afford. Most States will make it unlawful for an insurance company to sell a second Medigap policy to an individual unless that person cancels his or her other policy.

Medicare beneficiaries who are enrolled in HMOs and CMPs or are eligible for Medicaid usually do not need Medigap insurance. Fifteen States are expected to introduce Medicare SELECT in 1992 under a three-year evaluation by the Department of Health and Human Services. This is a private plan that is designed to offer the services of preferred providers, and will operate like HMOs, PPOs, and CMPs.

3. What Is The Difference Between Medicare And Medicaid?

DEAR MR. ANSWERMAN: Even though I am on Medicare, have private health insurance, and own my own home, can I still be eligible for Medicaid?

Dorothy K., Yakima, WA

STATES AND TERRITORIES PROVIDING MEDICAID TO THE "MEDICALLY NEEDY" AND THE "CATEGORICALLY NEEDY":

Arkansas   Utah
California   Vermont
Connecticut   Virginia
DC   Virgin Islands
Guam   Washington
Hawaii   West Virginia
Illinois   Wisconsin
Kansas
Kentucky
Louisiana
Maine
Maryland
Massachusetts
Michigan
Minnesota
Montana
Nebraska
New Hampshire
New York
North Carolina
North Dakota
Oklahoma
Pennsylvania
Puerto Rico
Rhode Island
Tennessee

DEAR DOROTHY K: To qualify as categorically needy for Medicaid, your income and assets must be at or below specific dollar amounts. States that provide Medicaid to the medically needy give coverage to those people whose medical expenses would bring their income and assets down to the State's elibility levels.

Basically, the answer to your question is yes, if you meet the Medicaid requirements in your State.

This can happen when your Social Security benefits are low enough that you become eligible for Supplemental Security Income (See "Knowing More About SSI" in this book).

Getting both Medicare and Medicaid can be helpful to those in need, since Medicaid would pay for some medical services that are not covered by Medicare.

Most states will let Medicaid pay the monthly premium charge by Medicare for Part B benefits.

The Medicare Catastrophic Coverage Act of 1988 requires state Medicaid programs to pay the Medicare premiums, coinsurance, and the deductibles for both the regular Medicare program and the new catastrophic insurance for those Medicare recipients who are also on Medicaid.

You can apply for Medicaid through your local Department of Social Services, Health Department, or Welfare Department. You can also apply at your Social Security office.

4. Does Medicare Cover Home Health Care?

DEAR MR. ANSWERMAN: I would like to know if Medicare covers Home Health Services and what is needed to provide for this kind of coverage? Would the same apply for Hospice Care coverage?

Edward P., Durham, NC

MEDICARE HOME HEALTH CARE COVERAGE:

--Visits limited to medically necessary
--Full cost of services
--80 percent for medical equipment
--Care must be approved by Medicare
--Must be physician approved

MEDICARE HOSPICE CARE COVERAGE:

--Available to terminally ill persons
--Up to 210 days if physician certified
--Outpatient drugs (some limits)
--Inpatient respite care
--Care must be approved by Medicare
--Must be physician approved

DEAR EDWARD P: If you need skilled health care in your home for the treatment of an illness or injury, Medicare pays for covered home health services that are furnished by a participating home health agency.

You must be homebound, need part-time nursing care, physical or speech therapy and under the care of a physician.

You can continue home health care for as long as you are under the doctor's care and the services are covered by Medicare.

Medicare pays the full approved cost of all covered home health visits. You will only be charged for services or costs that Medicare does not cover. If you need durable medical equipment, such as an oxygen tank, you are responsible for the 20 percent coinsurance payment.

For those who are terminally ill with a life expectancy of six months or less, hospice care is provided under Medicare. Patients must be certified by a physician and the facility must be approved by Medicare.

Under Medicare, hospice care is basically a home care program that provides medical and support services for the management of a terminal illness.

Thos who elect hospice care are not allowed to use standard Medicare to cover services for the treatment of conditions related to the terminal illness.

But standard Medicare benefits are provided for the treatment of conditions that are unrelated to the terminal illness.

There are special benefit periods for those who enroll in a hospice program.

5. How Do I Apply For Medicaid?

DEAR MR. ANSWERMAN: In addition to knowing how to apply for Medicaid, I would also like to know who is eligible for Medicaid, and how much income can I have and still be eligible for Medicaid? What about assets? Am I allowed to have any and how much?

Dudley Y., Warren, OH

COMBINED ASSETS RETAINED BY SPOUSES QUALIFYING FOR MEDICAID:

--A home in which the spouses live regardless of its value
--An automobile regardless of its value
--A wedding and engagement ring for each, regardless of its value
--Two burial plots
--Two savings accounts up to $1500 for each for burial costs
--Up to $6000 in property, like tools and equipment, used for support
--Life insurance with a face value up to $1500
--Assets varying from a low of $12,000 to a high of $60,000 depending on the State of residence

DEAR DUDLEY Y: To apply for Medicaid do so in writing to the State agency designated to handle Medicaid applications in your State. This is usually the Department of Social Services or Public Welfare. Some states allow you to apply at your Social Security office.

Eligibilty for Medicaid is based on poverty, but not all low-income persons are eligible. Your income and assets must be lower than the levels established by the State in which you live.

In most states, those who qualify for cash assistance from SSI are elibible for Medicaid. Other states use stricter guidelines and asset limits to determine whether or not a person is eligible.

Uner OBRA, the Omnibus Budget Reconciliation Act of 1986, states were given the option to expand Medicaid to cover incomes up to Federal poverty guidelines for those 65 and over, or disabled. In 1988, the poverty guidelines were $480.85 monthly for a single person and $644.17 per month for a couple.

The amount of income you are allowed also varies from state to state, the number of persons in your family, and other factors. The income rule is applied to mean that the income is "available" to you. An example is taxes you pay. These are not monies that are available to you and should not be counted as income.

Many of the states use SSI eligibility to determine income when considering Medicaid for a recipient. All your questions need to be specifically answered for you by someone in your state's Medicaid agency.

6. Can I Find Out Why I Was Turned Down By Medicaid?

DEAR MR. ANSWERMAN: I thought that I met all the eligibility requirements for Medicaid when I applied for it recently and I was shocked when I was turned down. All they sent me was a form letter and I have no idea why I was turned down.

Can you advise me how I can go about finding out why I was turned down?

Paul C., Livonia, MI

MEDICAID RESIDENCY REQUIREMENT:

--*U.S. Citizen*
--*Lawfully admitted aliens who are permanent residents*
--*Patients of a public or private mental hospital are not eligible for Medicaid between the ages of 22 and 65*
--*Residents in a public, nonmedical facility that is owned or controlled by the government are not eligible for Medicaid.*
--*You need not have lived in a state for any given period of time. The state must be your state of residence, though.*

DEAR PAUL C: Under Federal law you are entitled to timely and adequate notice of any decision to give you Medicaid benefits. You are entitled to written notice form the government that states what action it intends to take, the reasons for the action, the legal basis for the action, an explanation of your right to appeal the action, and an explanation of how you can get benefits while you appeal your case.

Federal law also requires that you get a fair hearing at which you can contest the decision to reduce, terminate or fail to process your application in a reasonable amount of time.

Submit a written request to the agency within ninety days of the date of the decision, telling them that you would like a hearing to contest the decision.

A conference can generally be requested or scheduled before your hearing to see if the problem can be solved without a hearing. But if you are not satisfied with the results of the conference, you still have the right to a hearing.

You may bring a friend, social worker, lawyer, or any other representative to help you at the hearing. You are allowed to testify at the hearing on your own behalf and you can cross-examine any witness the government presents at the hearing.

The hearing must be held at a location that is convenient for you. If you are homeboung or in a nursing home, you can insist that the hearing be held there.

If your case involves medical issues, you can have the medical exam at government expense to help you with your case.

7. Who Decides About Reasonable And Necessary Services?

DEAR MR. ANSWERMAN: Recently, I received several unpaid bills from Medicare with the explnation that they were not "reasonable or necessary" for the services rendered.

Could you explain what "reasonable and necessary" mean? I would also like to know what the differences are between custodial care and skilled nursing home care. Which one does Medicare pay and what can I do to cover myself on this?

Jessica S., Fort Myers, FL

DEFINITIONS:

REASONABLE AND NECESSARY --
services which the provider of the services decides are reasonable and necessary

UTILIZATION REVIEW COMMITTEES (URC) -- composed of
doctors and other medical personnel. They review admissions and stays in hospital and nursing homes to determine whether the patient requires the level of care offered in the facility.

HEALTH CARE FINANCING ADMINISTRATION (HCFA) -- administers the Medicare program nationwide

PEER REVIEW ORGANIZATIONS (PRO) -- determines whether the care to patients is reasonable and necesary

DEAR JESSICA S: All the factors defined under your letter are involved in deciding whether the services under Medicare are "reasonable and necessary." When HCFA or a PRO decides that services or costs provided by institutions or physicians were not "reasonable and necessary" they may refuse to pay them.

The appeals system, unfortunately, doesn't offer too many options to challenge a decision regarding financial liability for care. Many patients have had to leave a facility or decline treatment after being told their treatment is not covered by Medicare.

Your best advocate is your physician. If the doctor can give enough information, documentation, and reasons for the care, Medicare coverage is likely to be granted.

If you proceed with services that were found to be not "reasonable or necessary," you are likely to wind up with a bill that you are liable for and not Medicare.

If you were not informed that the services would not be covered by Medicare, when the provider offered them, you are less likely to be held liable for them.

This system, unhappily, has led many providers to deny services to those on Medicare when the program will not pay for them.

In cases where the patient has paid for services and is entitled to be reimbursed, he or she must submit a "Request for Indemnification" to Medicare. These forms are available from Medicare and Social Security offices.

8. What Is A Nursing Home?

DEAR MR. ANSWERMAN: Since Medicare and Medicaid are so careful in defining the treatment one can receive in a nursing care facility, I would like you to define for me, as precisely as you can, exactly what is a nursing home?

Also, who exactly runs nursing homes?

Patricia C., Lancaster, PA

TYPES OF NURSING HOMES: SNF — SKILLED NURSING FACILITY:

Provides skilled nursing care and related services or rehabilitation services to residents who are ill, but do not need to be in a hospital. They have medical directors who are physicians, and a nurse must be on duty 24 hours a day.

ICF — INTERMEDIATE CARE FACILITY

Provides health related care and services to individuals who do not require the degree of care and treatment which a hospital or skilled nursing facility is designed to provide. A nurse must be on duty 8 hours a day, seven days a week, but are not required to have a medical director.

PERSONAL CARE, BOARD-AND CARE, CUSTODIAL-CARE, DOMICILIARY-CARE FACILITY:

Provides room, board, and some physical help to residents in bathing, dressing, and toileting.

DEAR PATRICIA C: Today there are nearly 20,000 facilities in the United States that provide skill and/or intermediate nursing care to residents.

Only about 8 percent of these are owned and operated by the government. The rest are owned privately. About 22 percent are owned by nonprofit groups, like churches, while nearly 70 percent of nursing homes are operated for profit.

It is Medicaid and Medicare which has made it feasible for nursing homes to be in operation and even in some cases to become a big business.

If you want information about a specific nursing home, contact the nearest office of your state department of health and ask for the information. They are required to make available to you the names of the owners of a nursing care facility.

To check out their reputation, visit them and see for yourself what condition it is in and ask for some referrals. It is a good idea to talk to other people who have had direct experience with a nursing facility before using it for yourself or some one in your family.

There are nearly 1.5 million elderly Americans living in nursing homes. Most of them are over the age of 70, and women outnumber men three to one. Most of them suffer from several chronic diseases, like arthritis, heart disease, hypertension, impaired vision or hearing, and Alzheimer's. Many of them are very dependent. These are long-term residents.

Short-term residents are usually admitted after hospitalization for skilled nursing care.

9. How Expensive Are Nursing Homes?

DEAR MR. ANSWERMAN: I have heard a lot about how expensive nursing homes are. How effective are nursing home insurance policies in covering these expenses?

Are there any unlawful practices to watch out for?

Madeleine H., Macon, Ga

BUYER BEWARE:

--Companies willing to issue policies to someone over 85.
--Avoid policies that require hospitalization before a nursing-home stay.
--Avoid policies that require a prior level of care before benefits are payable.
--Read the policy carefully for definitions of level of care.
--Be sure it pays for all kinds of facilities, not just skilled-nursing care.
--Look for policies that seem less restrictive.
--Buy only one good policy.
--Upgrade the policy you have, don't buy a second, and third one.
--If your company won't upgrade, then shop for a new company.
--Keep your old policy in effect until you get your new one.
--Make sure someone you trust knows about your policy and where it is kept.

DEAR MADELEINE H: Nursing homes are often very expensive. A skilled nursing facility can cost over $4,000 a month. A lot depends on size and location of the facility and whether or not it is a skilled-nursing facility or an intermediate care facility, or simply a board-and-care one.

Before you or someone in your care goes to a nursing home find out what the costs are, including services like laudry, shampoos, and nonprescription drugs, like aspirin. Consider home health care as an alternative or a senior day care center.

Admission to nursing homes usually comes at a critical time in a person's life. Families are worried and concerned about getting the care the patient needs and considerations of costs come later.

Residents who are covered by Medicare and Medicaid are protected because of the controls written into their programs. Nursing homes that accept payment from these programs as payment in full, cannot collect extra sums from residents for services covered by the basic rate.

These homes cannot ask Medicaid eligible applicants, residents, or their families make contributions or other gifts to the home as a condtion of admission or continued stay in the home.

Medicaid patients are also not required to pay the rate charged by private paying residents for a period of time as a condition of admission.

10. Do Nursing Home Residents Have Rights?

DEAR MR. ANSWERMAN: I have read a lot and seen a number of programs on television about the abuses that take place in nursing homes.

How can nursing home residents be protected? What exactly are their rights?

Margaret W., Austin, TX

RIGHTS:

—*Personal liberty*

—*Privacy*

—*Speak freely*

—*Worship*

—*Information*

—*Adequate treatment*

—*Decline treatment*

—*See a doctor*

—*Control one's money*

—*To know the rules and rates of the facility*

—*Lawful contracts with the facility*

—*To information about the legality of "life-care contracts"*

—*Freedom of movement*

—*Freedom to leave*

—*Freedom to come and go*

—*Procedural protections before being transferred*

—*Resolution of disputes*

—*To take legal action*

DEAR MARGARET W: Nursing homes can provide residents with reasonable rules, but a person does not give up their legal rights when they enter a nursing home.

You are free to vote, marry, enter into contracts, practice your religion, complain, and see your friends just as you did before you entered the facility.

While states and the federal government have issued rules that are designed to ensure the rights of residents in nursing homes, they tend to be vague. In some cases, they can be overridden by a doctor.

The problem is that long-term care nursing home residents are usually not in a position to assert their rights, either because of their physical condition or the dis-orientation and memory loss that many suffer from.

In 1987 reform laws strenghtened residents rights by making it easier for states to monitor nursing home compliance and to punish noncomplying homes. An important provision is that nurses' aides must be trained to respect resident rights.

With facilities that are approved by Medicare, complaints against them can be taken to the regional offices of the Health Care Financing Administration of the U.S. Department of Health and Human Services. Others to contact are state, local and federal representatives.

There are some private consumer groups that serve as advocates and may be active in your area. You can also contact the State Aging Office in your area. Check the Appendix in the back of this book.

MEDICARE (PART A): HOSPITAL INSURANCE-COVERED SERVICES PER BENEFIT PERIOD (1)

Services	Benefit	Medicare Pays**	You Pay**
HOSPITALIZATION Semiprivate room and board, general nursing **and** miscellaneous hospital services and **supplies.**	First 60 days	All but $628	$628
	61st to 90th day	All but $157 a day	$157 a day
	91st to 150th day*	All but $314 a day	$314 a day
	Beyond 150 days	Nothing	All costs
POSTHOSPITAL SKILLED NURSING FACILITY CARE. You must have been in a hospital for at least 3 days and enter a Medicare approved facility generally within 30 days after hospital discharge. (2)	First 20 days	100% of approved amount	Nothing
	Additional 80 days	All but $78.50 a day	$78.50 a day
	Beyond 100 days	Nothing	All costs
HOME HEALTH CARE	Visits limited to medically necessary skilled care.	Full cost of services; 80% of approved amount for durable medical equipment.	Nothing for services; 20% of approved amount for durable medical equipment.
HOSPICE CARE Available to terminally ill.	Up to 210 days if doctor certifies need.	All but limited costs for outpatient drugs and inpatient respite care.	Limited cost sharing for outpatient drugs and inpatient respite care.
BLOOD	Blood	All but first 3 pints per calendar year.	For first 3 pints***

*   60 Reserve Days may be used only once; days used are not renewable.

**   These figures are for 1991 and are subject to change each year.

*** To the extent the blood deductible is met under one part of Medicare during the calendar year, it does not have to be met under the other part.

(1) A Benefit Period begins on the first day you receive service as an inpatient in a hospital and ends after you have been out of the hospital or skilled nursing facility for 60 days in a row.

MEDICARE (PART B): MEDICAL INSURANCE-COVERED SERVICES PER CALENDAR YEAR

Services	Benefit	Medicare Pays*	You Pay*
MEDICAL EXPENSE Physician's services, inpatient and outpatient medical services and supplies, physical and speech therapy,	Medicare pays for medical services in or out of the hospital.	80% of approved amount (after $100 deductible).	$100 deductible* plus 20% of approved amount (plus any charge above approved amount).**
HOME HEALTH CARE	Visits limited to medically necessary care.	Full cost of services; 80% of approved amount for durable medical equipment.	Nothing for services; 20% of approved amount for durable medical equipment.
OUTPATIENT HOSPITAL TREATMENT	Unlimited if medically necessary.	80% of approved charges (after $100 deductible).	Subject to deductible plus 20% of approved amount.
BLOOD	Blood	80% of approved amount (after $100 deductible and starting with 4th pint).	First 3 pints plus 20% of approved amount (after $100 deductible).***

* Once you have had $100 of expense for covered services in 1991, the Part B deductible does not apply to any further covered services you receive for the rest of the year.

** YOU PAY FOR charges higher than the amount approved by Medicare unless the doctor or supplier agrees to accept Medicare's approved amount as full payment for services rendered.

*** To the extent the blood deductible is met under one part of Medicare during the calendar year, it does not have to be met under the other part.

VII: KNOWING MORE ABOUT EARNED INCOME

1. What Is Self-Employment Income?

DEAR MR. ANSWERMAN: I am a medical writer working for a large pharmaceutical company. I have been employed with this company for the past eleven years, but have been thinking about going out on my own as a self-employed free-lance writer and editor in this field.

I would like to know if wages from self-employment are covered by Social Security. If they are, what are the rules that govern my earnings from self-employment?

Janette E., Mobile, AL

SELF-EMPLOYMENT MAXIMUMS:

$51,300...............1990
48,000.............1989
45,000.............1988
43,800.............1987
42,000.............1986
39,600.............1985
37,800.............1984
35,700.............1983
32,400.............1982
29,700.............1981
25,900.............1980
22,900.............1979
17,700.............1978
16,500.............1977
15,300.............1976
14,100.............1975
13,200.............1974
10,800.............1973

DEAR JANETTE E: Self-employment income means the net earnings from self-employment of a person for a taxable year.

The net earnings must be at least $400. The trade or business must be covered by Social Security. You must be a citizen or legal resident. Self-employed income greater than the amounts listed under your letter are not counted.

As you can see from the list, the amount of income that is counted has increased over the years and continues to rise automatically in multiples of $300. These are cost-of-living increases.

For the years prior to 1971 the maximum amounts were:

$9,000..........1972
7,800.....1968-1971
6,600.....1966-1967
4,800.....1959-1965
4,200.....1955-1958
3,600.....1951-1954

Net earnings, the amount you earn after you have computed your allowable expenses, that are greater than the maximum amount for a particular taxable year, are not considered self-employment income for Social Security purposes.

For the years before 1951, no maximum amounts are given, because self-employment was not covered by Social Security before 1951.

2. How Do I Report Tips?

DEAR MR. ANSWERMAN: I work as a waiter for a posh restaurant in San Diego. My tips come to a considerable amount by the end of the week. I have been getting information on how to report tips to Social Security and other tax returns, but the people I have been talking to don't seem to agree on how to handle this. Can you set me straight on this problem?

Ronald S., San Diego, CA

TIPS ON TIPS:

—*Tip reports must be timely.*

—*Tip reports must be complete.*

—*Employee's Social Security tax on tips reported to the employer will be deducted from wages.*

—*When employee's report to the employer is late or incomplete, employee must report directly to IRS.*

—*Employer is not required to pay Social Security taxes on tips employees receive, but must collect the Social Security tax due.*

—*Employers subject to minimum wage laws of the Fair Labor Standards Act may have to pay more Social Security tax.*

—*When employer cannot collect all the Social Security tax due on tips reported, employer must give the employee a statement of the tax still owed.*

DEAR RONALD S: The relationship between an employer and employee who receives tips is at the heart of how such tips are to be reported to IRS. The employer has some responsibilities and the employee also has some responsibilities.

Cash tips received by an employee after the year 1965 will count as wages for Social Security purposes if they total $20 or more in a month in the course of work for one employers. Such tips are subject to the payment of Social Security taxes.

Basically, you are expected to report your tips on or before the 10th day after the month in which the tips were received and they must be complete, including tips paid over by the employer when he/she receives them directly from customers.

There are forms that may be obtained from IRS for the use of employees in recording tips received, tip reports to the employer, and recording the dates and amounts of tips.

You can get them from your employer or the IRS. They are forms contained in Document 5635 and include:

Form 4070A - Employee's Daily Record of Tips

Form 4070 — Employee's Report of Tips to Employer

Employers sometimes use their own forms, but they must contain the same information as on Form 4070. Some employers have their employees report their tips on time cards or payroll forms. Be sure you are given a copy for your own records.

90

3. What Are The Tax Return Forms Used By Employers?

DEAR MR. ANSWERMAN: I have a small business with five employees. What are the tax return forms I need and what records should I keep for these workers?

Is there any other source of information on this subject that you would recommend?

Katee B., Ogden, UT

IRS PUBLICATIONS FOR EMPLOYERS CONCERNING SOCIAL SECURITY TAXES:

--*Publication 15, Circular E, Employer's Tax Guide for general employment.*
--*Publication 80, Circular SS, Federal Tax Guide for Employers in The Virgin Islands, Guam, and American Samoa.*
--*Publication 179, Circular PR (Federal Tax Guide for Employers in Puerto Rico)*
--*Publication 539, Withholding Taxes and Reporting Requirements.*
--*Circular A, Agricultural Employer's Tax Guide.*
--*Treasure Form W-2. This is the Wage and Tax Statement of earnings that must be given employees by every employer that is subject to Social Security taxes.*
--*Form 941. Employer's Quarterly Federal Tax Return.*
--*Form 942. Employer's Quarterly Tax Return for Household Employees.*
--*Form 943A. Employer's Annual Tax Return for Agricultural Employees.*

DEAR KATEE B: Please look over the publications I have listed under your letter and follow the instructions carefully that relate to your particular business.

Besides your obligations to file forms with IRS, you must be sure that the statements of earnings you give your employees are complete. Be sure they contain these items:

* Your name and address
* Your identification number
* The name and address of the employee
* The Social Security number of the employee
* The amount of wages, including tips, subject to Social Security taxes that were paid to the employee during the calendar year
* The amount of Social Security tax deducted from the employee's wages
* The total amount of tips reported to you that is subject to Social Security taxes
* The amount of Social Security tax, if any, the employee still owes on tips reported to you

This information must be given to employees no later than January 31 of the following year.

In your record keeping include names, addresses and occupations of employees receiving wages, their periods of employment, their Social Security numbers, the dates and amounts of each wage payment, and the amount of each wage payment that is subject to Social Security tax and the amount of tax that was withheld.

91

4. How Can I Get Help On Self-Employment Tax Payments?

DEAR MR. ANSWERMAN: I have been helping self-employed people with their taxes and I'm looking for more information to help my clients. Can you tell me some of the government publications that would help me in my business?

I am also helping someone who is trying to correct a Social Security earnings record. What do you recommend in this matter?

Jerry L., Green Bay, WI

SELF-EMPLOYMENT TAX PAYMENT PUBLICATIONS:

--*Publication 17, Your Federal Income Tax*
--*Publication 334, Tax Guide for Small Business*
--*Publication 553, Information on Self-Employment Tax*
--*Publication 225, Farmer's Tax Guide*
--*Publication 54, Tax Guide for U.S. Citizens Abroad*
--*Publication 595, Tax Guide for Commercial Fishermen*

FORMS:

--*FORM 1040. U.S. Individual Income Tax Return, including Schedule C (Famers use Schedule F)*
--*Schedule SE. Computation of Social Security Self-Employment Tax*
--*SSA-7004PC. Request for Statement of Earnings*

DEAR JERRY L: The list of publications under your letter will help you in your business.

You might want to help your clients further by getting a Social Security Summary Statement of Earnings for your clients. This can be done by using Form OAR-7014a. The summary will show the grand total of earnings credited and the annual totals of earnings for the four years preceding the current year. A benefits estimate is also shown on this form and your clients will appreciate this extra service in helping them plan their retirement, as well as their tax obligations.

There is no charge for this information and you can serve as the authorized representative for your clients.

To correct a Social Security earnings record, you need to get in touch with the nearest office which will check to see if any missing reports of earnings can be located. It may be necessary for the Social Security office to contact past employers to get this information.

If your client has records to substantiate a claim of an incorrect earnings record, the job of correcting the record is much easier.

Be aware and make your clients aware that there is a time limit to correcting records. An earnings record can be corrected at any time up to three years, three months, and fifteen days after the year in which the wages were paid or the self-employment income was derive.

Ater this period of time the records can only be revised to correct an entry if fraud or mechanical error can be established.

5. Should I Or Shouln't I Retire?

DEAR MR. ANSWERMAN: Aside from knowing how to shelter my earnings after I retire, I would like to know about the wisdom of working after retirement. Some people say they can't wait to get out on the golf course, while I hear others say they hate the thought of being "put on the shelf" at retirement. What is your opinion?

Jean Ann M., Norwalk, CT

TITLES TO LOOK FOR IN YOUR LIBRARY:

--Job Hunting After Forty
--Transferability of Vocation Skills
--40 million Americans in Career Transition
--Handbook of Job and Career Opportunities
--Industrial Gerontology
--What Color Is Your Parachute?
--Where Do I Go From Here With My Life?
--Career Change
--Guide to Starting a Business
--Educational Gerontology
--Second Careers
--Second Wind: Handbook for Happy Retirement
--Life Work Planning
--Life Cycle Planning
--Second Chance: Blueprints for Life Change
--On Your Own: 99 Alternatives to a 9 to 5 Job
--Work, Aging, and Social Change

DEAR JEAN ANN M: Many people who reach retirement age do not retire, but instead they start a new career.

Many researchers who study older populations believe that persons as they age beyound sixty-five are much the same as they were in middle age. They have the same psychological and social needs they had before retirement.

This "activity" approach to senior years recommends that retirees keep active, find other work that they like, and not let themselves be put on the shelf.

The other school of thought on aging is that a person should disengage from their former activities, because older people want less social interaction.

As far as I'm concerned, I think this is a matter of personal preference. If you want to keep active after retirement, you may want to look into a new career, perhaps something you have always thought of doing, but put off because of time and commitment to a job or your family.

One of the great benefits to our Social Security system is that it allows you some leisure to reorient yourself for your "golden years." If you want to spend them on the golf course, that's fine. If on the other hand, you want to be productive and still feel capable of working in an employment situation, you might want to explore the possiblity of starting a small business of your own.

I recently had the experience of finding a cat sitter for my two cats. The lady I hired started this business with a handful of business cards and some flyers.

6. How Many People Over 65 Still Work?

DEAR MR. ANSWERMAN: Since I plan to keep working after 65, I am curious to know how I stack up against the general population statistics in this category.

Rose L., Tyler, TX

STATISTICS OF OLDER AMERICANS:

--Median income > $13,107 for males
$ 7,655 for females
--10.7 million family households have median income of $23,179
--9.4 million nonfamily household have median income of $9,638
--Major source of income >
Social Security (39%)
Asset Income (25%)
Earnings (17%)
Pensions (17%)
Other (3%)
--Subsidized housing > 27%
--Medicaid coverage > 12%
--Median net worth > $60,300
--Poverty level > 3.4 million older persons
--Near poor > 2.3 million
--One-fifth of older population poor or near poor
--States with highest poverty rates for older persons > Mississippi (34%); Alabama, Arkansas, Louisiana (28%); Georgia (26%); South Carolina, Tennessee (25%); Kentucky (23%)

DEAR ROSE L: There are about 3.4 million older Americans in the labor force, which is about 12 percent of that population. You are not alone, but you are definitely in a minority.

Of this figure, 2 million were men and 1.4 million were women. They make up less than 3 percent of the U.S. working population.

While at the beginning of this century, nearly two-thirds of the male population over 65 were still working, by 1985 less than 16 percent were in the labor force. Since then the rate of employment among older men has increased to 16.6 percent in 1989.

In 1900 only about 8 percent women over 65 worked, but by 1956 this figure rose to nearly 11 percent of that group. The figure fell to about 7 percent in 1956, but rose again by 1989 to over 8 percent.

Of the older workers employed, more than half were only employed part time, especially among women.

Self-employment among older workers is much higher than among younger ones. Only 8 percent of younger workers are self-employed, while 25 percent of older workers are self-employed. The figure is 824,000. Seventy-five percent of that figure are men.

Older people are interestingly becoming better educated. In the past two decades the median level of education has increased from 8.7 years to 12.1 years of education. More than 54 percent were high school graduates and about 11 percent had 4 or more years of college.

7. Can I Get Tax Counseling?

DEAR MR. ANSWERMAN: I am collecting Social Security, working part time, collecting from a pension, and other capital investments, but I'm still not in the league where I can afford a tax accountant.

Is there any way I can learn more about taxes or is there someone or a group to help seniors with their taxes as a free service?

James B., Decatur, GA

FREE TAX PUBLICATIONS:

--Guide to Free Tax Services
--Your Rights as a Taxpayer
--Tax Information for Military Personnel
--Student's Guide to Federal Income Tax
--Your Federal Income Tax
--Farmer's Tax Guide
--Tax Guide for Small Business
--Tax Guide for Commercial Fishermen
--Federal Estate and Gift Taxes
--Tax Information for Divorced or Separated
*   Individuals*
--Medical and Dental Expenses
--Exemptions, Standard Deduction, and
*   Filing Information*
--Moving Expenses
--Taxable and Nontaxable Income
--Credit for the Elderly or the Disabled
--Recordkeeping for Individuals
--Pension and Annuity Income

CALL IRS TOLL-FREE AT:

1-800-829-3676

DEAR JAMES B: The first thing to do to get free help with your taxes is to call the toll-free number listed in the left-hand column under your letter. Ask IRS to send you a copy of Publication 910, *Guide to Free Tax Services.*

IRS offers free tax services in the form of its publications, toll-free telephone assistance, Tele-Tax -- a recorded tax information and automated refund information line on 140 topics, telephone tax assistance for the hearing impaired, braille materials for the blind, and walk-in service.

Assistors at IRS offices will walk through a return with a group of tax payers in a group setting. You can get many tax publications and forms off the rack in most IRS offices, as well.

In addition to this help from IRS, there are a number of volunteer and education programs they sponsor. To get more information call your local IRS office and ask for the Taxpayer Education Coordinator.

Among the type of volunteer programs you might encounter is the Community Outreach Tax Education, which offers both line-by-line income tax return preparation and tax seminars on specific tax topics.

Volunteer Income Tax Assistance (VITA) Program provides free help to people with basic tax returns. Tax Counseling for the Elderly (TCE) provides free tax help to people aged 60 or older. You may also come across Small Business Tax Education Programs and Student Tax Clinics that offer free help. These are held in convenient community locations.

8. Can I Afford To Not Work After Retirement?

DEAR MR. ANSWERMAN: What with the cost of living rising each year and real estate getting higher, even with a pension and some other income, do you think it is still a good idea to continue to work? I'm wondering if I work now when I still have the strength and health to do so, if I won't be better off in the long run.

Arlene B., Abilene, TX

SPECIAL FIRST-YEAR RULE:

—*During the first year of your retirement the special first-year rule allows you to get the full amount of your retirement benefits for any month in which you do not earn more than the maximum allowable, which is $570 if you are between 62 and 64, and $780 if you are 65 to 69.*

—*Self-employed may receive full benefits for any month in which they do not perform more than 45 hours of service during the month.*

TAXES ON SOCIAL SECURITY BENEFITS:

—*For most people retirement benefits are tax-free. IRS does not consider Social Security income. You do pay tax on interest you earn from savings however.*

—*If your income adds up to $25,000 or more ($32,000 for a couple), you pay income tax on half your SS benefits.*

DEAR ARLENE B: Many people keep working when they start collecting Social Security and their pensions, not only for economic security, but also to remain an active participant in the world of work.

But take into consideration the fact that working may reduce your Social Security retirement benefits. Do some careful calculations before you make your final decision. You must figure what the maximum is that you can earn within a month without losing benefits. Social Security will not count any money you receive from such things as insurance premiums, investments, pensions, rental income, royalties, or savings.

In 1990, if you were under 65 you were allowed to earn $6,800 per year of earned income without having your beneftis reduced. The limit is $9,360 for those between 65 and 69. Once you are over the age of 70, you may earn as much as you are able to without any reduction in your Social Security benefits.

After the cut-off level, onc dollar of your benefits will be taken away for each two dollars you earn over the amount allowed.

The best way to handle this if it is your situation is to tell Social Security in advance so that you do not receive over-payments and have to repay them later. You want to avoid a situation where you have spent money that you must later return.

Once you report earnings to Social Security they will make periodic requests that you report any changes. If you stop working, report this to begin collecting your maximum Social Security benefit.

9. How Does Social Security Know About My Earnings?

DEAR MR. ANSWERMAN: I have recently retired and begun receiving Social Security benefits, but I am continuing to work on a part-time basis. My part-time work is self-employed work that I do at home on a contract basis with my former employer.

Do I have to report my earnings to Social Security or do they just pick up this information from my Federal Income Tax Returns? Or is this the responsibility of my employer even though we are working in this new arrangement?

Lester R., Richmond, VA

EXCESS EARNINGS ARE CHARGED AGAINST:

--The retired individual
--Cause deductions from the total monthly family benefit including the spouse and children

EXCESS EARNINGS ARE NOT CHARGED AGAINST:

--Disability insurance benefits
--Benefits of an entitled divorced spouse who has been divorced from the retired person for at least two years

DEAR LESTER R: The Social Security Administration requires that you submit a report each year predicting your monthly and annual earnings.

They will ask those who are most likely to underestimate their earnings in a given year to report to them semiannually. If the report predicts excess earnings, benefits will be reduced or suspended until the excess has been collected.

A second report may be required at the end of the year if no original report was filed or if the original report was inaccurate. For instance, a person might have earned more or less than predicted in the original report.

Social Security does check with the Internal Revenue Service to make sure that earnings reports are accurate and to catch people who earn money but fail to file a report with the Social Security Administration.

As a result of the second report or the check with IRS, Social Security may decide that a person has been overpaid in months when excess earnings occurred. When this happens, Social Security will try to collect the overpayment by reducing future benefits. They may even terminate them.

Reporting your earnings to Social Security is primarily your responsibility, not your former employer, especially since you are working on a contract basis. Your retirement is really in your hands and you must deal with the Social Security Administration. As a self-employed person, you are now responsible for your Federal taxes and your Social Security benefits.

10. What If Social Security Says I Have Been Overpaid?

DEAR MR. ANSWERMAN: I need some help in dealing with Social Security. They claim that they have overpaid me because I was working part-time last year, but my records show that I did not have "excess earned income" in any one month. I believe they have lumped together some of the money I earned in one month with another month. This is giving me quite a lot of trouble.

What are my rights and how do I go about protecting them?

Ann Marie C., Jamaica, NY

TERMS TO KNOW AND UNDERSTAND:

--*At Fault. Social Security considers you "at fault" if you give them an incorrect statement concerning eligibility for benefits, failed to give information you knew was important, or accepted payment that you knew was incorrect.*
--*Recovery Against Equity and Good Conscience. This occurs when your financial situation changes making it a hardship to repay Social Security.*
--*Recovery Defeating the Purpose of the Social Security Act. When you can establish that you have limited income and assets and need Social Security benefits to meet the ordinary and necessary expenses of life.*

DEAR ANN MARIE C: The first thing to do is to get an appointment to discuss the situation with a Social Security official. If you disagree with them and your talks end in a stalemate, you can appeal this determination by using the normal appeals procedures. See Chapter 1, Question 8 in this book for some details on the appeals procedure.

Social Security wants repayment of overpaid benefits. They can suspend your checks until the overpaid amount is recovered or they can reduce your monthly checks and recover the overpayment over a longer period of time.

They cannot, however, recover an overpayment if you were not at fault in allowing the overpayment, which means you did not deliberately give them misinformation.

They also cannot recover an overpayment if it would cause you an undue economic hardship because of your present circumstances or because it might defeat the purpose of Social Security.

If you have good evidence of your case and can show them through pay stubs that their information is incorrect, you should have no trouble.

You have the right to a personal conference on the issue of request for recovery of overpayment. Don't let grass grow under your feet though. You must do this quickly, because Social Security has time limits under which they operate. You have thirty days to ask for a reconsideration or waiver on notice of an overpayment.

VIII: TAX CREDITS AND DISABILITY

1. Who Must File A Return?

DEAR MR. ANSWERMAN: I keep hearing about special tax breaks that older persons are entitled to on their Federal income tax returns. Both my wife and I are over 65 and together we earn less than $10,000, not counting Social Security. Do we still have to file an income tax return?

Greg R., Boston, MA

CHART OF PERSONAL EXEMPTIONS:

Status	*Age*	*1988 Gross Income*
Married	*Both Under 65*	*$8,900*
	One Spouse Over 65	*9,500*
	Both Over 65	*10,100*
Surviving Spouse	*Under 65*	*6,950*
	Over 65	*7,550*
Household Head	*Under 65*	*6,350*
	Over 65	*5,700*
Single	*Under 65*	*4,950*
	Over 65	*5,700*
Married Filing Separately		*1,950*

DEAR GREG R: By all means file a return, even if you owe no tax. You may still be entitled to a refund.

The chart in the left-hand column will help you locate your status and gross income. It would seem from what you say in your letter that you will not have to pay any tax.

Your filing status plays an important part in deciding whether or not to file a return. It determines what tax rate schedule you should use.

There are five separate status categories for filing -- single, married filing jointly, married filing separately, qualifying widower, and a head of household.

For purposes of determining marital status the key date is December 31 of the tax year for which you are filing. This question often comes up when retired people over 65 enter into a new marital arrangement.

Persons who were never married, were divorced, or legally separated on that date are considered single. Those who were married on December 31, even if they were living apart without a legal separation, are considered married for Federal tax purposes.

Widows and widowers who do not remarry for the tax year may still file a joint return for that year and two more years if you remain single and have a dependent child.

2. What Are Exemptions?

DEAR MR. ANSWERMAN: My elderly mother is living with me. Even though she is receiving $4,000 in Social Security benefits, can I still claim her as an exemption?

Beatrice W., Des Moines, IA

GUIDELINES FOR CLAIMING DEPENDENT PARENTS AS AN EXEMPTION:

--If you pay more than 50 percent of the parent's actual living expenses, you may claim them as dependents.

--If you are unmarried, you may claim a filing status as head of household, rather than filing as a single person.

--You may add medical expenses of your dependent parent and deduct what is in excess of 7.5 percent of your adjusted gross income (this may change each year).

--You may give taxable stocks and bonds to a parent rather than sell them and pay tax on possible capital gains. Interest or dividends from these can be used for a dependent parent's support. The tax rate will be lower for a person over 65 than for you.

DEAR BEATRICE W: What you have to determine is whether or not you are paying more than half of your mother's support.

Since she is receiving $4,000 in Social Security benefits, you need to determine if you are paying more than that to qualify to claim her as a dependent.

Your mother must have an income less than the annual exemption ($2,000 in 1989), not counting Social Security or SSI beneftis. She must also be an American citizen and not have filed a joint return with a spouse for that year.

Food, clothing, shelter, medical and dental care are considered support. You may be able to value her room at $250 a month, which comes to $3,000 a year. You can calculate food costs at $30 a week, which would come to about $1500 a year. These two items alone add up to $4,500 a year, which is more than her $4,000 income from Social Security.

The other expenses of clothing and medical and dental care can also be estimated into your computations. You should have proof of these expenses, so it is a good idea to keep grocery receipts, rent or mortgage payment receipts or cancelled checks for all the items that you use to calculate your expenses in caring for your mother.

Your exemption for her as your dependent will be a fixed amount. It was $2,000 in 1989, with an adjustment for inflation beginning in 1990.

3. What Are Special Tax Breaks?

DEAR MR. ANSWERMAN: I understand that there are certain kinds of income that still qualifies for favorable tax treatment. Could you list them and describe the tax advantages each one receives?

Mary Lou H., Evanston, IL

SPECIAL TAX TREATMENT INCOME:

--*Life Insurance Proceeds. These are not subject to income tax, but the interest from them when you take the proceeds in installments over a period of time is subject to taxation.*
--*Employee Death Benefits. Up to $5,000 of an employer death benefit does not count as income.*
--*Injury or Sickness Compensation. This type of income does not count as income. You do not have to pay income tax for worker's compensation benefits, money received from a personal injury lawsuit, or payments from an accident or health insurance policy for which you paid the premiums.*
--*Sale of Personal Residence. You can postpone payment of income tax on the capital gain of you home if you buy a new home within two years before or after the sale of the personal residence. If the new home does not cost more than the old one, you will be taxed only on the difference of the adjusted sales price.*

DEAR MARY LOU H: Income as it is defined by IRS is all income received from any source, whether it is money, property, or services.

Gifts and inheritances, happily, are not considered income, therefore items that fall into those categories are not taxed as income.

Life insurance proceeds, employee death beneftis, compensation for injuries or illness, and the sale of a personal residence all fall into the category of special treatment by IRS.

When selling a house you can deduct costs like real estate broker's commissions, selling expenses, and expenses to make the property saleable, such as repairs and repainting.

You can also add into the cost of your new home cash payments, mortgages, commissions, purchase expenses, and capital improvements made two years before and after the sale.

Homeowners over the age of 55 receive another special tax break. They do not have to pay income tax on $125,000 of capital gain. Both spouses must agree to claim this tax break, since it can be used only once per couple. If either spouse has previously claimed this special tax break, then the other one cannot claim it. This can become a problem in situations where a second marriage has occurred.

There is a special form to file with IRS. It is Form 2119. Save this form to help you keep track of your home's tax basis. It will help to get hold of **Publication 523, "Tax Information on Selling Your Home"** from your local IRS office.

4. Should I Itemize Deductions?

DEAR MR. ANSWERMAN: Could you please explain the difference between standard and itemized deductions? How can I use these deductions as I grow older to my advantage? What about taking care of a disabled person?

Shirley F., Columbia, SC

STANDARD DEDUCTION CHART:

Joint or Surviving Spouse	*$5,000*
Head of Household	*4,400*
Single Persons	*3,000*
Married, Filing Separately	*2,500*

ITEMIZED DEDUCTIONS:

--*Charitable Contributions. List on Schedule A of Form 1040 cash, gifts, and services to qualified charitable and religious organizations.*

--*Medical Expenses. Only those that exceed 7.5 percent of your adjusted grow income may be deducted.*

--*Interest Deductions. You may deduct interest paid on mortgages and home equity loans. Personal interest, such as on car loans or credit cards is no longer deductible.*

--*Vacation Homes. Annual taxes and mortgage interest are deductible.*

DEAR SHIRLEY F: I will answer the last question about the disabled in the next few questions.

Before you decide whether to take the standard deduction or to itemize your deductions, take a look at your assets and where your expenses are coming from. If you own a house and are paying a mortgage, it is usually more advantageous to itemize deductions.

Even with the standard deduction, a married person or surviving spouse who is either blind or over 65 is entitled to another $600 in the standard deductions. If the person is both over 65 and blind, the deduction is $1,200. An additional standard deduction of $750 is allowed for an unmarried (single) person over 65 or blind. Therefore, persons in this category may be able to deduct up to $1,500 on the standard deduction. These will be adjusted for inflation and may be higher when you take it, if it is after 1989.

People over 65 who are claimed as dependents on another person's tax return, may claim a special standard deduction of either $500 or an amount equal to their earned income, up to a ceiling of $3,000, whichever figure is higher.

In cases when itemized deductions are greater than the standard deduction for the year, then itemizing deductions will be the best route for a person to take.

There are ceilings on the amount of mortgage interest that a homeowner can take as a deduction. As of 1988, $1,000,000 was the limit and $100,000 was the limit on home equity loans. An advantage to home equity loans is that the money can be used for any purpose.

5. Are There Special Credits For The Elderly And The Disabled?

DEAR MR. ANSWERMAN: Please tell me how much my income limit has to be to get a special tax credit and which IRS forms I need to use. I am 67 years old.

Debra E., Beaumont, TX

INCOME LIMITS CHART FOR SPECIAL TAX CREDIT FOR ELDERLY AND DISABLED:

Status	Adjusted Gross Income	Nontaxable Income
Single	$17,500	$5,000
Married, Joint Return, Both Eligible	25,000	7,500
Married, Joint Return, One Eligible	20,000	5,000
Married, Separate Return	12,500	3,750

DEAR DEBRA E: You qualify because of your age.

People who are either disabled or over 65 may claim a special tax credit if they meet the income limits shown in the table on the left under your letter.

The value of a tax credit for people with limited incomes is valuable because they can deduct it directly from their tax bill, while tax deductions are only subtracted from their adjusted gross income.

The amount of the credit cannot be more than your tax bill, though. To file for this credit use IRS Form 1040 to claim it. You cannot claim it on 1040EZ or 1040A.

This credit is available only to the elderly and disabled whose adjusted gross income or nontaxable retirement or disability benefits fall below the limits listed in the chart.

If you are over 65 and have to pay income tax on your Social Security of Railroad Retirement benefits, your income is probably too high to qualify for this credit.

Sometimes disabled persons who are under the age of 65 must meet special rules to calculate this credit. They should complete Schedule R and attach it to the 1040 tax form.

6. Is There Credit For Dependent Care?

DEAR MR. ANSWERMAN: I would like to find out more about the tax credit for dependent care. Could you tell me the ceilings on this credit and some of the conditions that limit claiming this credit? Also, what are the conditions for an earned income credit?

Lewis G., Hampton, VA

CONDITIONS FOR DEPENDENT CARE CREDIT:

--*You and your spouse (unless spouse is disabled) must be working.*

--*The dependent must be your spouse or another person who is incapable of caring for him or herself, or a child under the age of 15.*

--*The person must be your legal dependent.*

--*The dependent must live with you.*

--*You must pay one half of the household expenses.*

--*The expenses for taking care of the dependent must make it possible for you to work full or part time.*

--*These expenses may include the cost of hiring a cook, maid, or attendant.*

DEAR LEWIS G: Dependent care credit is designed to help those who work take care of their dependents who cannot care for themselves.

You may claim credit for this type of care in your home or a day care center to help cover some of your expenses.

You must meet the conditions I have outlined in the left-hand column of this page. In addition, there are ceiling limits to this credit.

The first ceiling allows you to count expenses of no more than $2,400 per year for one dependent and $4,800 for two or more dependents.

The second ceiling limits the expenses to the amount of income earned by either you or your spouse, whichever is lower. If your spouse doesn't work, you cannot claim the credit. If your spouse is disabled then the spouse can be treated as if they had earned $200 a month or $400 for two or more dependents.

The third ceiling allows you to claim only 20 to 30 percent of dependent care expenses. This depends on your income.

If your "earned" income is below $18,566, you may also be eligible for earned income credit. You must be married and entitled to a dependency exemption for a child living with you, or a qualified widow or widower, or the head of a household entitled to a dependency deduction for a child living with you. The maximum earned income credit was $875 in 1988. In some cases you may even receive a payment if your credit is greater than your tax liability.

7. What Are The Disability Benefits For Older Persons?

DEAR MR. ANSWERMAN: I am 62 and disabled. Should I go on Social Security, or are there disability programs for which I should first apply? What is my best course of action?

Carl P., Jackson, MS

DISABILITY PROGRAMS UNDER THE SOCIAL SECURITY ADMINISTRATION:

--*Supplemental Security Income (SSI). This pays benefits to disabled persons provided that their countable income and resources are below a certain level.*

--*Social Security Disability Insurance Program (Title II of the Social Security Act). This pays benefits to disabled workers, widows, widowers, adn their dependents provided the worker is fully insured.*

DEFINITION OF DISABILITY:

--*An inability to engage in any substantial gainful activity by reason of any medically determinable physical or mental impairment which can be expected to result in death or which has lasted or can be expected to last for a continuous period of not less than 12 months.*

DEAR CARL P: Generally, it is advisable to apply for Social Security disability benefits rather than for early retirement if you are unable to work.

The first reason is that your benefits are likely to be higher. Social Security under the disability program will pay an individual the same benefits that he or she would receive if the person were to retire at age 65.

Under early retirement benefits are reduced by five/ninths of one percent for each month of retirement before one's 65th birthday.

There are special earnings requirements that have to be met to qualify for Social Security disability benefits. You could have enough quarters to qualify for early retirement, but you may not meet the special earnings requirements for Social Security disability benefits.

A person who receives disability beneftis for a period of 24 months becomes eligible for Medicare.

In many states the SSI program is tied to the state Medicaid program. For this reason it is advisable to also apply for SSI benefits. The cash benefit may not be as helpful as this medical one.

For widows, widowers, and surviving divorced spouses, there is an actuarial reduction. A person can receive as low as 71.5 percent of the benefit he or she would otherwise receive if the person had waited until the age of 65 to take the benefit.

Approximate Monthly Benefits If You Become Disabled In 1991 And Had Steady Earnings

Your Age	Your Family	Your Earnings In 1990					$51,300
		$10,000	$20,000	$30,000	$40,000	$50,000	Or More[1]
25	You	$473	$ 732	$ 958	$1,079	$1,196	$1,202
	You, your spouse, and child[2]	687	1,098	1,437	1,619	1,795	1,803
35	You	468	722	950	1,069	1,174	1,177
	You, your spouse, and child[2]	674	1,083	1,426	1,604	1,762	1,766
45	You	467	720	947	1,040	1,103	1,105
	You, your spouse, and child[2]	672	1,081	1,421	1,560	1,655	1,657
55	You	469	724	934	997	1,040	1,041
	You, your spouse, and child[2]	676	1,086	1,402	1,496	1,561	1,562
64	You	476	736	942	997	1,035	1,036
	You, your spouse, and child[2]	690	1,104	1,414	1,496	1,553	1,554

[1] Use this column if you earn more than the maximum Social Security earnings base.
[2] Equals the maximum family benefit.
Note: The accuracy of these estimates depends on the pattern of your actual past earnings.

106

8. How Is Disability Determined?

DEAR MR. ANSWERMAN: My brother-in-law told me the other day that claiming a disability with the Social Security Administration is not easy. He says that I should get legal help if I plan to apply. Is he right?

Edward V., Troy, NY

STEPS SOCIAL SECURITY TAKES TO DETERMINE DISABILITY:

—*Step One. Is claimant engaged in Substantial Gainful Activity (SGA)? If Yes, the benefits are denied. If No, claimant goes to Step Two.*

—*Step Two. Does claimant have an impairment expected to last at least 12 months or end in death? If Yes, claimant goes to Step Three.*

—*Step Three. Does the impairment significantly limit the ability to work? If Yes, claimant goes to Step Four.*

—*Step Four. Does the impairment meet or equal a listing (see Question 9, following for a definition)? If Yes, a benefit is awarded. If No, claimant goes to Step Five.*

—*Step Five. Does claimant have capacity to return to past work? If Yes, claim is denied. If No, claimant goes to Step Six.*

—*Step Six. Is claimant able to do any SGA in the national economy? If Yes, benefits denied. If No, benefits awarded.*

DEAR EDWARD V: You might do well to listen to your brother-in-law. The process for applying for disability benefits is complicated and the support you get from legal advocates that are experienced in this area of law can help you analyze and process your case properly.

When Social Security evaluates Substantial Gainful Activity, they look at experience, skills, supervisory functions, and responsibility. They consider how well you do your work, whether it is done under special conditions, and how long it takes you.

They also consider the amount you earned in the evaluation, your age, education, and work experience.

In one part of the process, Social Security will gather information about the type of work you have done in the past fifteen years. They pay particular attention to the amount of exertion the jobs required, the skill levels of the jobs, the tools and machinery that was used, the degree of responsibility you had, and the degree of supervision under which you worked.

Before denying benefits Social Security must show that you can do some work in light of your age, experience, and education.

There is also an exception to the step-by-step process. Those with marginal education who have 35 or more years of arduous unskilled labor experience and cannot perform their former work are generally considered disabled. Coalminers and some construction workers might fall into this category.

9. What Are The "Listings"?

DEAR MR. ANSWERMAN: I've been told that the Social Security Administration uses a list of impairments to determine whether or not to award a claim. Does this mean that only certain disabilities qualify for disability benefits? Can you give me some information about these "listings"?

Henry S., Akron, OH

THE BODY SYSTEMS UNDER WHICH IMPAIRMENTS ARE CATEGORIZE FOR ANALYSIS TO CLAIM DISABILITY BENEFITS:

—*Musculoskeletal System*
—*Special Senses and Speech*
—*Respiratory System*
—*Cardiovascular System*
—*Digestlve System*
—*Genito-Urinary System*
—*Hemic and Lymphatic System*
—*Skin*
—*Endocrine System*
—*Multiple Body Systems*
—*Neurological System*
—*Mental Disorders*
—*Neoplastic Diseases, Malignant*

NOTE: These listings are found in Appendix 1 of the Social Security regulations which contain a "Listing of Impairments."

DEAR HENRY S: Most disability applicants have their claims evaluated in light of the listings in Appendis 1 of the Social Security regulations.

Disabled widows, widowers, and disabled surviving divorced spouses must show that their impairments meet the listings or are equivalent to a listing.

Failure to meet the requirements of the listings does not necessarily mean that a claim will be denied. Claims are analyzed according to the guidelines of the step-by-step process that Social Security follows.

The listings were revised and updated in 1985 with the mental impairment listings expanded substantially to bring the regulations more in line with the current views for analyzing mental impairments.

There are actually two sets of listings. One applies to those over the age of 18 and the other to those under the age of 18. Each set of listings are categorized into thirtecn body systems, which I have listed in the left under your letter.

In addition to these thirteen, children are analyzed for the category of growth impairment.

Because the analyzing of impairments is a highly specialized one, it is necessary to get professional medical and legal help to be sure than a correct analysis is made.

It is not an easy job to compare a person's particular disability against the "listings." These judgments are highly complex and need expert medical and legal opinions.

10. What Are The "Grids"?

DEAR MR. ANSWERMAN: I am 56 years old with an 8th grade education. I was a furniture mover before I injured my back and I can no longer do that kind of work.

How will Social Security handle my case? Will they make me do some other kind of work? I don't think I can do any heavy work any more, like manual labor. And I also think I couldn't even work in a fast food restaurant, because I can't stand on my feet all day because of my back. What do you think my chances are of getting on disability?

Roger B., Pontiac, MI

FACTS ABOUT THE "GRIDS":

--Formerly called "Medical-Vocational Guidelines"
--Grids formalize claimant's age
--Grids formalize claimant's education
--Grids formalize claimant's work experience
--Grids are tables based on a claimant's Risidual Functional Capactiy (RFC)
--RFC determines the limitations of work claimant is capable of doing
--Used by Social Security in cases where an individual has established the inability to return to former work
--Used by Social Security in cases where impairments are mostly exertional

DEAR ROGER B: I think your chances of getting Social Security disability benefits are probably pretty good. But I would advise you to get some expert help to help you process your case.

Your work should be categorized as heavy work. If it is found that you are not capable of performing medium work, which would required you to lift up to 50 pounds occasionally and 25 pounds frequently, then the medium work table of the grids would be applied to your case.

Since your age is considered advanced and your education is marginal, and in light of your prior work experience, rule number 203.01 would apply to your case. This rule directs a finding of disabled.

The "grids" have to be viewed with caution, since nonexertional impairments, like mental problems, sensory and skin problems, posture and manipulative limitations, pain, and environmental factors, like the inability to tolerate dust or fumes, are frequently ignored by Social Security.

In these cases, the claimant needs to document his or her case carefully and thoroughly.

Social Security needs to show that jobs exist in significant numbers in the national economy that the claimant can perform before it can deny benefits.

The grids are only relevant when one has established an inability to return to one's former type of work. Social Security has been known to misapply the grids inappropriately. A person may have a high school education, but may be functionally illiterate, thereby not qualifying for a job that uses those skills.

IX: FIGHTING AGE DISCRIMINATION IN EMPLOYMENT

1. Is Age Discrimination In Employment Illegal?

DEAR MR. ANSWERMAN: A friend of mine was recently denied a promotion and then given an early retirement by the company he has worked for many years.

He is 56 and thinks that the company discriminated against him because of his age. Are there any laws that would protect him?

Bruce F., Brooklyn, NY

FEDERAL LEGISLATION THAT PROTECTS PERSONS AGAINST AGE DISCRIMINATION IN EMPLOYMENT:

--*Title VII of the Civil Rights Act of 1964. Prohibits discrimination based on race, color, religion, sex or national origin. Section 715 of Title VII includes recommendations from the secretary of labor for legislation to prevent arbitrary discrimination in employment because of age.*

--*Age Discrimination in Employment Act of 1967 (ADEA). Enforcement originally fell to the secretary of labor.*

--*Equal Employment Opportunity Commission (EEOC). Authority to enforce ADEA was transferred to EEOC in 1979.*

DEAR BRUCE F: Discrimination on the basis of age in employment is illegal under the laws of many states, as well as under the Age Discrimination in Employment Act of 1967 (ADEA), which is enforced by the Equal Employment Opportunity Commission (EEOC) at the Federal level.

ADEA prohibits covered employers from discriminating against job applicants and employees in hiring, promotion, training, demotion, lay off, fringe benefits, and firing.

ADEA also makes it illegal for employment agencies to discriminate on the basis of age in employment referrals. It is illegal for labor organizations to discriminate against their members on the basis of age. The law also prohibits age-based employment advertising.

In times of recession, many companies need to reduce their work force and the temptation to target older, higher-paid employees has been hard for employers to resist and hard for older employees to fight.

Proving that you were not hired because of your age is also not easy to do. But the situation may change over the next several decades, since the number of younger workers entering the job market is declining. Businesses may find that older workers are well-suited for the kind of jobs that will need to be filled in our technological society.

2. Who Is Protected By ADEA?

DEAR MR. ANSWERMAN: I have been reading about the Age Discrimination Act (ADEA) and I would like to know more about who is protected by this legislation, especially in terms of age groups.

Are certain kinds of work exempted from the ADEA? In other words, what kind of employers are subject to the ADEA?

Barbara S., Spokane, WA

WHO ADEA PROTECTS:

--All individuals over the age of 40
--All Federal employees over the age of 40
--Applicants for employment
--Employees of any employer covered by the law
--U.S. citizens employed by a U.S. employer or by a foreign company controlled by a U.S. employer in a workplace located in a foreign country

EXEMPTIONS:

--State and local governments until 31 December 1993 for law enforcement officers and firefighters
--Tenured faculty until 31 December 1993
--Elected state and local officials
--Non-civil service staff
--Policy-making government employees
--Executives who retire with benefits equal to $44,000 per year may be retired at 65

DEAR BARBARA S: People who feel that they have been discriminated against in employment because of their age have to know what protection they have under their particular state laws and what protection the ADEA offer.

Some state laws protect a wider range of people or may prohibit only particular age-based conduct. ADEA does not preempt state or local laws or regulations that prohibit age discrimination in employment.

There is a growing body of law, based on common-law contract theories, that offers the basis to challenge age discrimination in employment when the law does not specifically grant rights.

Courts have recognized good faith and fair dealing in employment relationships in decisions regarding age discrimination.

Anyone considering an age discrimination case should determine if their state has a law prohibiting age discrimination in employment and whether it has an agency to enforce such a law.

When this is the case, a claimant must use the state administrative proceeding before bringing a lawsuit based on ADEA. This procedure has already been decided at the Supreme Court level.

Because these are difficult cases, it is wise to receive some help. A good place to start is to contact the agency in your state that deals with aging. You can find a list of these agencies in Appendix IV of this book.

3. How Can Discrimination Be Proven?

DEAR MR. ANSWERMAN: I applied for a job at a machine shop plant and was turned down, even though I had the qualifications and the work references.

While applying for the job, I was given their employer's personnel manual. It stated that any person under 21 or over 50 would not be eligible for a job. I am 52. Do I have a case of age discrimination?

Victor J., Charleston, WV

WHERE TO FIND EVIDENCE FOR AGE DISCRIMINATION IN EMPLOYMENT:

—*Job descriptions*

—*Work rules*

—*Personnel pamphlets or manuals*

—*Company notices*

—*Job advertisements*

—*Statements by company officials*

—*Statements by supervisors*

—*Statements by personnel employees*

—*Any verbal statement by management that suggests age discrimination*

AREAS OF PROOF OF AGE DISCRIMINATION:

—*Lack of valid reason for not getting a job or promotion*

—*Evidence the position went to a younger, less qualified applicant*

DEAR VICTOR J: The only way to make a case of age discrimination is with evidence showing that the employer explicitly relied on the age of the applicant or employee in making a decision.

The case you cite is a clear case of age discrimination. I hope you kept the manual if you decide to take a case against this employer.

It is possible even without written evidence to establish that an employer is engaged in age discrimination in hiring, promotions, and lay-offs.

In these cases the claimant must show that different treatment, "disparate treatment," occurred to the protected group, which is those over the age of 40.

If an employer refuses to offer training to employees or hire those over 50, that employer is discriminating on the basis of age. Once it is shown that an employer has discriminated on the basis of age, the employer has to show a nondiscriminatory reason for its actions.

An important indication that an employer is discriminating is when an applicant who is over 40, is qualified for the job, was rejected, and after being rejected, the employer continues to seek applications with the claimant's qualifications.

In circumstances like these, it is possible to have the basis for a case of age discrimination. Some cases of age discrimination become complicated because there may be more than one reason for the dismissal, non-hiring, or lay-off of the employee.

4. Are There Other Standards For Age Discrimination?

DEAR MR. ANSWERMAN: Since a new supervisor has been hired at my job, I have been having a lot of trouble. He is a younger man who is always telling jokes about older people and making snide remarks about their inability to perform the job.

My boss says there is simply a personality conflict between us and wants to let me go. I say it's age discrimination. Do I have a case?

Pamela R. Cincinatti, OH

BASIS FOR DISPARATE IMPACT CLAIMS OF AGE DISCRIMINATION IN EMPLOYMENT:

--Employment policies that appear to be neutral, but have a greater negative impact on those over 40
--Not hiring a person with more than two or more years of experience
--Job-related employment qualifications that include a level of physical fitness that may eliminate more older people from job opportunities
--Demotions based on being at a higher pay scale
--Seniority factors used to lay-off, demote, or transfer employees
--Special training needed and not offered to those over 40
--Firing older workers to replace them with younger ones because they offer more potential to the employer

DEAR PAMELA R: You need to document the remarks that this new supervisor is making and, if possible, get one or two other employees to sign your record of the remarks.

Using the excuse of a "personality conflict" is an old game that many employers play when they simply don't want to face the truth about a situation that involves discrimination.

You should make it clear that you want to keep your job and that you have no wish to leave the job.

While ADEA allows employers to act on reasonable factors other than age, asking you to leave because of a "personality conflict" seems like a poor excuse to let you go. Your employer is also neglecting to take into account the obvious prejudice of your new supervisor in persistently telling jokes that make fun of older people and imply they are unable to perform the work.

You could ask for a transfer. It would be unlawful for your employer to deny you a transfer on the grounds of your age. If this happens, it would strengthen your case of age discrimination.

Whether a company uses age-based reasons to offer employment to new employees or uses age as an excuse to squeeze out older employees, the company is engaging in unlawful age discrimination. Your supervisor's behavior toward you and your boss's suggestion that you leave seem to clearly indicate that your age is being used against you.

5. Are There State Laws Prohibiting Age Discrimination In Employment?

DEAR MR. ANSWERMAN: Are there ever any advantages in filing an age discrimination case through a state law rather than through ADEA or EEOC?

Do all states have agencies that deal with this problem?

Judith T., Billings, MT

REASONS FOR FILING WITH A STATE AGENCY IN AN AGE DISCRIMINATION CASE:

--Some state laws offer greater protection than the Federal agencies
--Some state laws cover workers who are younger than 40
--Some state laws protect employees who work for employers with fewer than 20 employees
--State agencies may investigate cases quicker
--State agencies may make the process easier
--Some state agencies are more aggressive about prosecuting age discrimination cases
--State agencies may not be as overburdened with cases as the EEOC and ADEA

DEAR JUDITH T: If you check in Appendix IV of this book, you will find an agency in your state to contact for information about filing a case in your state.

The state laws do vary from place to place. You may choose to file a complaint under state law or under federal law, or both.

Many people have found that it is easier, quicker, and more convenient to file with their state, rather than with the EEOC, because they get better results. One always has the advantage when dealing with a local agency that can be contacted more easily and quickly, than one that is centered in Washington.

Some states, though, have only laws, but no agency to enforce the law. In these cases, the person filing the complaint has to use the federal law or resort to a private lawsuit.

In most cases, you will be asked to file a written complaint, most likely on a form that the agency will give to you. The agency will contact your employer and try to mediate your complaint. Your employer will have a chance to present his or her view of the situation.

If the agency decides that your complaint is not valid or can't be proved, they may decide to drop the case. But if they find that you have a valid complaint, they will try to negotiate a compromise. If this fails, a hearing may be held in front of an administrative judge or board. That decision can then be challenged by you or the employer in state courts.

6. How Do I File An Age Discrimination Complaint?

DEAR MR. ANSWERMAN: I would appreciate it if you could give me the step-by-step procedures on how to go about filing an age discrimination suit.

I was recently discharged from my company after 25 years of service. I feel that I was forced to take an early retirement because of my age. For the past several years my company has been pressuring many of its employees into taking early retirement. They either eliminate the jobs or hirer younger people to fill them at much lower salaries and without the special benefits we had been getting.

Harry W., Fort Wayne, IN

PROCESS OF FILING AN AGE DISCRIMINATION CASE:

—*Gather your information.*
—*Locate assistance through a state aging agency.*
—*File a complaint with your employer.*
—Contact EEOC and your state agency.
—*Discuss the problem with both agencies.*
—*Decide who will be most helpful.*
—*File a complaint with EEOC and the state agency.*
—*Interview by agency with employer*
—*Formal investigation*
—*Agency files a lawsuit on your behalf*
—*Private lawsuit filed by you*

DEAR HARRY W: ADEA has established procedures to insure that you get all the protection that the law offers you.

You must first file a complaint with your employer, which means following the company's own established grievance procedures. At this step the company may rectify the problem without your having to take the complaint any further. This will certainly be less trouble than going all the way to court, if your case can be resolved at this level. Even if you think it is hopeless, you must give it a try. Anyway, you must take this step before EEOC or your state agency will handle your complaint.

If you belong to a union file a grievance with the union. Some unions have been doing an excellent job handling age discrimination cases. There may be staff workers who can help and there may also be a legal fund to help with the costs involved in the case.

If nothing is resolved, then file with both your state agency and EEOC, but file with one earlier than the other on the basis of which one you think will prosecute your case more aggressively. The other agency will wait to see the outcome before they get involved, but you have them as a back up. You will need to have filed with both your state agency and EEOC before you can take your case to court under the guidelines of ADEA, anyway, so this should be done.

There is a time limit of 180 days to file with EEOC from the date of the action of your complaint.

DEAR MR. ANSWERMAN: I have been told that I should write a letter to the EEOC agency in my state to make a formal charge of age discrimination in employment.

What are some of the other procedures I should follow?

Chuck N., Chicago, IL

WHAT YOUR LETTER TO EEOC SHOULD INCLUDE:

--*Your name*
--*Your address and zip code*
--*The date of the letter*
--*Re: Age Discrimination in Employment Charge*
--*The name of your employer*
--*The address and zip code of your employer*
--*State that the letter is a formal charge of age discrimination*
--*State your job title*
--*State the length of time of your employment with the company*
--*State your age*
--*State the nature of your complaint*
--*Give exact dates of examples of discrimination*
--*Give exact details of examples of discrimination*
--*Be specific about the age discrimination events*
--*Give the names of any management personnel involved in your charge*
--*State what action you have taken in bringing your complaint to the attention of the company*

DEAR CHUCK N: After filing with EEOC, you will be notified by mail to make an appointment to see an investigator. The EEOC investigator will ask you questions during your interview about details of your charge. The investigator will examine your evidence and ask you what outcome you are hoping for.

The EEOC investigator will open a file on your charge. If you have witnesses to back up your charge, be sure to give their names to the investigator. It is helpful to supply a detailed list of the events that led you to take your case.

The investigator will contact your employer and ask for information about the company's position on the charge. The investigator will arrange a meeting between you and your employer in the presence of an EEOC official.

Compromises are often reached at this stage. If not, a formal investigation will follow if EEOC feels the case merits it. This could take weeks or months. EEOC will continue to try to convince your employer to settle your case.

If the case cannot be settled this way, EEOC may refer the case to the U.S. Department of Justice to consider filing a lawsuit in federal court on your behalf against your employer.

The Justice Department, however, chooses only those cases in which there is both a chance of winning and in which the decision by the courts would impact a large number of workers. You can still pursue your case through your state agency or through a private lawsuit, also.

8. When Do I Take
A Private Lawsuit?

DEAR MR. ANSWERMAN: I would like more information on filing a private lawsuit after I take my case to EEOC, in case they fail to win my case. How expensive are lawyers going to be in these kind of cases and what are my chances of winning such a case?

Forrest V., Tulsa, OK

WHERE TO LOOK WHEN HIRING A LAWYER:

--Choose a lawyer who is experienced in age discrimination cases.

--Contact your local lawyer's referral panel of your local bar association for a referral to a lawyer who specializes in age discrimination cases.

--Contact senior citizen organizations in your community to find names of competent lawyers for your case.

--Contact the state agency on aging in your state for a referral.

--Contact the National Organization for Women (NOW). Many age discrimination cases involve older women.

--Contact the Commission on the Status of Women. They deal with age and sex discrimination and will know lawyers who handle these cases.

--Ask the clerk's office of the United States District Court to make a referral.

DEAR FORREST V: Before you file a private lawsuit, find a competent lawyer who has experience handling age discrimination cases.

You may not file a lawsuit in federal court until at least 60 days after you have filed a complaint with EEOC. If your state has an agency that enforces its own age discrimination laws, you must wait 120 days after you file your state charge or until the state case is dismissed.

But you must file your federal lawsuit within two years from the date of the act of age discrimination you claim took place. The exception to this limitation is in cases where you can prove that the discrimination was willful.

Lawyers who specialize in age discrimination cases may be willing to take your case on a contingency basis, which means they will wait to get paid from the final court award or settlement of your case. When a lawyer accepts a case on this basis, he or she generally believes there is a good chance of winning the case.

You may be asked to pay for some of the expenses, such as filing fees, when a lawyer accepts your case on a contingency basis. Lawyers have been more willing to take this kind of case on this basis, since more of them are being heard before a jury and they are usually more sympathetic than the judge might be.

If you win, your legal fees may also be paid by the defendent, your former employer.

9. Is There Protection Against Discrimination From Government Services?

DEAR MR. ANSWERMAN: I am a member of a minority group and I feel I have been treated in a prejudicial manner by my local unemployment agency.

I am also in my late fifties. Who should I contact to discuss this problem with?

Rosalind O., Atlanta, GA

AGENCIES TO CONTACT TO FILE DISCRIMINATION FROM GOVERNMENT AGENCIES:

--United States Department of Labor
Directorate of Civil Rights
200 Constitution Avenue, NW
Room N-4123
Washington, DC 20219

--The local Office of Equal Opportunity in your community

--The local Department of Labor office in your community

--Any social service agency in your community that defends discrimination for your minority group and/or age discrimination

DEAR ROSALIND O: If you feel you have been denied participation in or benefits from Unemployment Insurance or Job Service on the basis of race, color, national origin, sex, age, religion, political affiliation, belief, citizenship, or participation in programs funded in whole or in part by the Job Training Partnership Act of 1988.

Claimants of the Job Service and Unemployment Insurance programs are also protected from discrimination on the same basis.

You have the right to file a complaint of discrimination not later than 180 days from the date of the alleged discriminatory act. You may bring your complaint to the attention of the Local Office Manager of the agency which discriminated against you in an attempt to resolve your charge.

The agency is required to issue a determinaton on your complaint within 60 days of the date on which you file your complaint.

If the complaint is not resolved withing 60 days, or the agency's determination is not satisfactory to you, you may file with the Directorate of Civil Rights (the address is in the left-hand column of this page) withing 30 days of the agency's decision or 90 days from the date of the filing, whichever is earlier.

10. If I Win A Case, Will I Receive Back Pay?

DEAR MR. ANSWERMAN: Could you tell me what someone who wins an age discrimination suit could expect in back pay awards and compensation for pain and suffering?

Shelly B., St. Louis, MO

TERMS IN SETTLEMENTS:

--*Back Pay. Compensation for all wages and other monetary benefits lost as a result of discrimination*
--*Hiring. Courts have the authority to require employers to hire victims of discrimination.*
--*Reinstatement or Front Pay. Courts have the authority to provide equitable relief, including reinstatement.*
--*Promotion. Under ADEA the courts have authority to grant judgments compelling promotion to individuals wrongfully denied promotions.*
--*Liquidated Damages. Where a violation was willful, victims of discrimination are entitled to liquidated or double damages. This could occur in cases where the employer is found to show reckless disregard to the law.*
--*Preliminary Injunctions. An employee can get an injuction against an employer who may be threatened with retirement. The court can forbid the action until the case is heard.*
--*Attorney's Fees and Costs. Courts may award these.*

DEAR SHELLY B: The basic principle underlying remedies to age discrimination is that the victims should be restored to the economic position they would have occupied had the employers not intervened unlawfully.

Yes, if you win your case you will be entitled to back pay. The purpose of ADEA is to promote employment of older persons based on their ability rather than their age. The act prohibits arbirary age discrimination in employment.

Among the forms of relief that courts may grant under ADEA is to compel the employer to employ the person discriminated against, reinstatement when the employee was laid off or fired or forced to retire, promotions, juddgments enforcing liability for amounts owing as a result of violations of the act, which includes back pay, benefits, and other relief.

As far as pain and suffering, there have been very few cases won in federal court, but there have been some awards at the state level. You may do better to file with your state agency if you feel you have suffered severe emotional distress, especially if it has led to medical problems and costs.

An individual who has been unlawfully discharged, the usual award is all lost wages until the time of reinstatement by the employer and other monetary benefits, such as pension benefits, health benefits, insurance, sick leave, and seniority rights.

The other items listed in the left-hand column are also awards that might be made in age discrimination cases.

X: ESTATE PLANNING

1. What Is The Importance Of Estate Planning?

DEAR MR. ANSWERMAN: While I don't have a very large estate, I do have a substantial amount of assets that I will be leaving behind after my death.

I know that I can't take it with me and that someone else will be enjoying these assets. But I would like to assert some control over how these assets will be used.

What is the approach you recommend?

Andrew F., Hartford, CN

CONSIDERATIONS IN ESTATE PLANNING:

--Decide who you want to inherit your assets.
--Determine how much of your estate is needed to give your spouse an adequate income.
--Decide who will manage your estate.
--Decide whether or not to keep or sell your home.
--If you keep your home, decide what to do with the mortgage.
--Decide about leaving assets to others besides your spouse.
--If you leave assets to more than one person, decide what needs you what to cover.
--Decide about leaving assets to charities or causes.

DEAR ANDREW F: You can control what happens to your assets after your death by planning now how you want them used and to whom they are to go.

First decide who you want to inherit your assets. If you have a spouse, you will want to provide for her living expenses, especially if she is in poor health or disabled.

You may also have children or grandchildren with special needs and want to leave them something to help them when you are no longer there.

Basically, you will make your decisions on the basis of what you would be doing if you were still alive.

Your largest asset may be your home. If you die, you must decide if it would be best for your wife to be able to continue living in the home and whether there will be enough in the estate you leave her for her to continue to maintain the home. If you still have a mortgage on the home, you might consider paying it off to reduce its maintenance when you are no longer there to pay for it.

You will also have to consider whether your heirs -- your spouse or others -- will be able to manage your estate. You will have to assign some as the trustee to your estate. Should that be a family member, a friend, or a professionally managed one?

These decisions should all be made while you are still in good health .

2. How Do I Make An Inventory Of My Property?

DEAR MR. ANSWERMAN: Are there special forms I should use to help me figure out what I have and how I should distribute my assets after my death?

Duane P., El Paso, TX

CASH FLOW STATEMENT:

--Income. Include monthly income from all sources, such as salary, dividends, interest, rental income, business income, annuities, social security.

--Expenses. Include mortgage payments, rent, utilities, telephone, maintenance, repairs, services, taxes, insurance, loan payments, food, clothing, medical, entertainment, charitable contributions, and all other fixed and variable expenses on a monthly basis.

--Total each column of items. Subtract your expenses from your income, which gives you your current net income (income after expenses).

DEAR DUANE P: You don't need a special form. Just sit down with paper and pencil and make a list first of all your monthly income. Be sure to list everything. If you are getting quarterly dividends on stocks, average them out on a monthly basis.

The first column of this list will be your current income. Next to it list what you expect your income to be after retirement.

When you have taken stock of your monthly income, current and future, then list your monthly expenses as they are now. With items that are variable, like repairs, average them out over a year to get an approximate monthly figure. Then list what you expect your monthly expenses will be after you retire.

By subtracting your expenses from your income, you can see what your net income is and will be when you retire.

The cash flow statement will give you a good picture of your current and future financial situation and help you decide how to plan your estate for your heirs.

A net worth statement (a form is included on the next page) will help you make a complete inventory of your assets and your liabilities. This in turn will help you decide whether you should dispose of your property and assets through a will or through a trust.

The advantage of a trust is that you can maintain lifetime rights to income from your assets and they are distributed according to the terms of the trust. If you don't have a will or a trust, the state in which you live will dispose of your property according to a formula.

Net Worth

Assets -- What We Own	Bill and Nancy	Your Figures
Cash:		
Checking Account	$ 800	_____
Savings Account	4,500	_____
Investments:		
U.S. Savings Bonds (Current cash-in value)	5,000	_____
Stocks, mutual funds	4,500	_____
Life Insurance:		
Cash value, accumulated dividends	10,000	_____
Company Pension Rights:		
Accrued pension benefit	20,000	_____
Property:		
House (resale value)	50,000	_____
Furniture and appliances	8,000	_____
Collections and jewelry	2,000	_____
Automobile	3,000	_____
Other:		
Loan to brother	1,000	_____
Gross Assets	**$108,800**	_____

Liabilities -- What We Owe

	Bill and Nancy	Your Figures
Current Unpaid Bills	600	_____
Home Mortgage (remaining balance)	9,700	_____
Auto Loan	1,200	_____
Property Taxes	1,100	_____
Hoime Improvement Loan	3,700	_____
Total Liabilities	**$16,300**	_____

Net Worth: Assets of $108,800 minus liabilities of $16,300 equals $92,500.

DEAR MR. ANSWERMAN: I would like to know at what point my estate would have to pay federal taxes and how that tax is computed.

Can you detail some of the items that I need to consider to help my plan my estate? I would like to conserve as much of my estate as possible to give me security during retirement and also want to leave a good sum to my family when I die, so I am concerned about my tax obligations and how they might reduce my overall assets.

Douglas D., Covington, KY

COMPUTING FEDERAL ESTATE TAXES:

--List the items in your gross estate.
--List their values.
--Subtract allowable deductions. This is the taxable estate.
--Add any taxable gifts given after 1976. This is your tax base.
--Multiply the tax base by the applicable tax rate. This is the tentative estate tax.
--Subtract unified credit.
--Subtract credit for state death taxes paid.
--Subtract any other credits.
--You will have your net estate tax.

DEAR DOUGLAS D: The federal estate tax is imposed after the death of a person whose estate exceeds $600,000.

You may think that your estate is not valued that high, but when you add up your savings, your pension fund, life insurance, stocks, real estate, and other real property, you may find that your estate is valued greater than $600,000.

This is how the gross value of your estate is determined. All real estate or personal property that you own alone, such as house, car, furniture, and jewelry, is counted. Debts owed to you, the value of an annuity that you have been receiving, such as a pension or IRA, life insurance proceeds, property recived from your spouse, gifts of property made to others worth more than $10,000 in a single year are part of your gross estate.

The face value of life insurance policies that are transferred withing three years of your death is counted, not the cash value.

Jointly owned property is counted in several ways. If you hold it with your spouse, only half its value is counted into your estate, but the entire value of the property you own jointly with someone else is counted, minus that person's contribution to its value.

In a community property state, the entire value of any property you received by gift or inheritance is counted into the gross value of your estate.

An alternative date, usually six months after death, is sometimes chosen to establish the fair market value of property in your estate.

4. What Deductions Can I Use On My Federal Estate Tax?

DEAR MR. ANSWERMAN: Could you list the deductions on the federal estate tax and itemize what those deductions include?

I would also like more information on credits, especially the unified tax credit? Which of these deductions and credits will help the most in reducing estate taxes?

Betty H., San Francisco, CA

PERMISSIBLE DEDUCTIONS FOR FEDERAL ESTATE TAXES:

--*Funeral expenses includes the costs of a tombstone, monument, mausoleum, burial plot, perpetual care, transportation, and any other related costs.*
--*Adminstration of the estate. This includes attorney, accountant, appraiser, and executor fees, plus paying off debts and costs in collecting assets.*
--*Claims against the estate. Unpaid debts, mortagages, and income tax may be deducted.*
--*Losses due to casualties and theft while settling the estate that are not reimbursed by insurance.*
--*Charitable gifts to religious, scientific, educational, literary, or government may be deducted.*
--*Gifts to a surviving spouse.*

DEAR BETTY H: The deductions that I have listed under your letter may be subtracted from your gross estate. This reduces the amount of your estate and thereby the amount of your tax.

When you subtract your deductions from your gross estate, what is left is your tax base. Let's say that your tax base is $550,00 after deductions and your tentative tax is $203,500.

All decedent estates are entitled to the unified credit, which cancels the first $192,800 of the estate tax liability. In this case it reduces the estate tax to only $10,700.

There are also credits for previous estate taxes that were paid on an estate. If the beneficiary of the estate dies within ten years partial or full credit can be claimed on the estate that was left to the newly deceased person.

Gift taxes that were paid before 1977 may also claim a credit if it was included in the gross estate. For property owned in a foreign country, the U.S. allows a tax credit for that property.

You are also entitled to a certain amount of credit on your federal estate tax for any state death taxes that the estate must pay. State taxes apply to real estate owned within the state, tangible person property like furniture, and intangible property like stocks and bonds.

The unlimited deduction for gifts to a surviving spouse can be quite complicated. It is not always classified as "no strings attached." This should be discussed thoroughly with a professional before

5. What Is A Gift Tax?

DEAR MR. ANSWERMAN: I am 72 years old and plan to reduce the taxes on my estate as much as possible. I have two adult children and six grand children.

How can gift-giving reduce my federal estate tax when I die? Please explain how this can be arranged. Also, how can my estate benefit from the generation-skipping transfer tax?

Marlene S., Trenton, NJ

GIFT TAX LIMITATIONS:

—*$10,000 per person in one year.*

—*No limits on the number of persons.*

—*May be given each year.*

—*Spouses may claim the marital deduction for gifts to each other no matter what the amount.*

—*Tuition paid directly to a school or college for someone else is deductible.*

—*Medical expenses paid directly to the provider on behalf of someone else.*

—*Generation-skipping transfers have a $1 million lifetime exemption.*

DEFINITION:

—*Generation-skipping Transfer Tax. The transfer of property to a person two or more generations younger you may avoid possible estate tax on the generation skipped.*

DEAR MARLENE S: Giving gifts is a good way to reduce a large estate during one's lifetime. Considering your age, this is something you may want to do if you have an estate that will be heavily taxed when you die.

You will have the satisfaction of seeing the happiness you bring to the persons you choose to receive your gifts while you are still alive. Many people with large estates do this in their planning. When these gifts are made, you must report them to the IRS in the year in which you make the gifts.

There is a tax penalty for gifts over $10,000 given to an individual in a single year. But this can be avoided by simply giving only $10,000 each year to the person. You can repeat this gifting year after year and you can give to as many persons as you choose.

You and your spouse, if he is also living, may each give $10,000 to each person without being liable for the gift tax.

Spouses may give one another larger sums, but your spouse will be liable for the tax when he or she dies.

Gifts to tax-exempt organizations, like charities, schools, and religious institutions are also not taxed. You may want to include these in your estate planning.

For very large estates, tax planners have been advising people to consider the Generation-Skipping Transfer Tax. With this tax you can avoid estate tax on the next generation, your children, and skip to the next generation, grandchildren. This can be very complicated and you should get the advice of a tax expert to clarify it for your particular situation.

6. What Are Gifts To A Spouse?

DEAR MR. ANSWERMAN: What are some of the advantages and the risks of gifting one's spouse to save on inheritance taxes? Do the same advantages and risks apply to children as well?

Marion C., Anderson, IN

CAUTIONS ABOUT GIFTING TO SPOUSES OR CHILDREN:

—*Shifting liability of income to a spouse does not reduce taxes when filing a joint return.*

—*You lose adjusted gross income exemptions of $25,000 for older single persons or $32,000 for couples if you file separate returns and are collecting Social Security benefits.*

—*The recipient of property given as a gift must pay taxes on the full capital gain of the property if they sell it.*

—*Gifting a jointly owned family residence before death may result in a higher capital gain for the surviving spouse.*

—*The donor spouse may die before the recipient spouse.*

—*The recipient may divorce the donor.*

—*Children under age 14 who receive gifts may be taxed at your rate.*

—*Gifting to children may make it difficult for their parents to claim them as deductions.*

DEAR MARION C: Whether you are thinking about gifting some of your assets to your spouse or your children, you need to get some expert tax advice. These are very complicated situations for estates and there are situations that you need to avoid, because you can end up paying more, rather than less tax.

I have listed some of the precautions to keep in mind when gifting.

There are several situations in which gifting to a spouse can result in tax savings. One situation is when one spouse has extremely high medical expenses that are not being reimbursed either by Medicare or a private health insurance policy. If income is transferred to the spouse with high medical expenses, the assets can be used to pay the medical bills and that spouse can claim a deduction. The other spouse then has a lower tax rate, because he/she has reduced income.

In states with high tax rates couples can file separate returns and pay a lower state income tax than filing a joint return.

Jointly owned property in most cases is best held jointly until the death of one of the spouses.

Gifts to children under the age of 14 will result in little income tax savings if the child receives annual income from the gift. Good gifts to give to young children are growth stock, which increases in value after the child reaches age 14, and Series EE Savings Bonds, which will mature after the child reaches age 14.

7. What Is The Language Of Wills?

DEAR MR. ANSWERMAN: I've noticed that a lot of special legal terms are used when making up a will. Can you give me a list of the important ones?

David K., Falls Church, VA

TERMS USED IN WILLS:

—*Conditional Will. States intention if an uncertain event happens.*

—*Holographic Will. Written, dated, and signed in the person's own handwriting.*

—*Joint Will. The will of two or more persons, jointly signed.*

—*Joint and Mutual Will. Created jointly by two persons, providing that the surviving person receives all the assets, and after the death of the surviving spouse the assets go to other parties.*

—*Self-Proved Will. Eliminates some formalities of proof in the probate of a will.*

—*Living Will. States the wishes of the person about life-sustaining treatment in case of physical or mental disability.*

—*Estate. Total property of any kind that you own.*

—*Probate. Court procedures to prove a will valid or invalid.*

—*Testator. A person who makes a will.*

—*Personal Representative or Executor. The person you appoint to carry out the directions of your will.*

DEAR DAVID K: More important than knowing about the language of wills is knowing that it is important to have a will, even if you have named beneficiaries in insurance policies and pension benefit plans that you might have. Even when you have a trust, it is a good idea to make out a will, because without a will the state in which you lived will decide how to dispose of your property.

Generally this means that your assets pass to your spouse and your children, but instead of you deciding what share they get, the state makes that decision.

In cases where there are no spouse or children, your assets will be portioned out to your parents, siblings, or other relatives. If you have any concern about where your money should go when you die, you should make out a will. You do not necessarily even have to see a lawyer to make out a will. Forms are sold in book stores and stationery shops and you can draft and sign the will yourself. Be sure to follow the instructions carefully, though, and be sure you get valid witnesses to sign your will.

If you have a large and complicated estate, you may do better to seek professional help. Among other things it is important to know what the special arrangements are in your particular state. You can, of course, check this out on your own by visiting your public library or a law library in your area. Whether you use a lawyer of not, educate yourself completely to be sure that your will carries out your wishes.

8. How Do I Create A Will?

DEAR MR. ANSWERMAN: My family has been after me to make a will. It all seems so complicated. Can you simplify the process for me so that I'll be more inclined to get one made up?

Bonnie I., Philadelphia, PA

REQUIREMENTS FOR CREATING A WILL:

--You must be 18 (usually).
--You must understand what you are doing.
--You must sign the end of the will, unless you are unable to. Then someone may sign for you in your presence.
--You should initial each page of the will.
--Make a statement at the signing that this is your will, that you know its contents, and that it expresses your wishes.
--Have witnesses sign the section of the will that attest that you executed this with full knowledge of the contents of the will.
--Have the witnesses sign a separate affidavit that declares the witnesses are of the opinion that you had the mental and physical capacity to make the will at the time of the signing.

DEAR BONNIE I: It is easy to create a will. If you are fairly young or have a simple and modest estate, a form type will may well be all that you need.

What you really need is the will to create a will. It is a good move, since it protects your interests and the interests of those you love and care about.

Check about the affidavit of self-proof that states require of witnesses. There may be a special form in your state. The purpose of this special affidavit is that most states accept this in place of the testimony of the witnesses when questions of the validity of the will come up.

The affidavit eliminates the need for witnesses to appear before the court or make sworn statements should there be a dispute.

While in most cases only two witnesses are needed to attest to a will, it is a good idea to have an extra person in case one dies or cannot be located because the person may have moved. It is also a good idea to have the people who witness your will be younger than you.

It is necessary to have only an original copy of a will, but it is helpful to have an extra copy.

It is not a good idea to keep it in your safe deposit box at a bank, because it will be sealed at your death and cannot be opened except by a court order. You can keep it in a fire box at home or have your attorney or a friend or relative that you trust hold it for safe keeping.

9. Can A Will Be Changed?

DEAR MR. ANSWERMAN: I prepared a will over twenty years ago, and lately I have been thinking that I should probably change my will. Will this be a complicated thing to do? And how do I go about doing it? It has been so many years that I forget what the whole process was like.

Richard E., Augusta, GA

WHEN TO CHANGE YOUR WILL:

—*When you marry.*
—*When you divorce.*
—*When you have a child.*
—*When you have additional children.*
—*When there is a substantial change in the amount of your estate.*
—*When the nature of your assets change.*
—*When you move.*
—*When you retire.*
—*When you inherit some assets.*
—*When your children marry.*
—*When you become a grandparent.*
—*When you want to leave something to a person not mentioned in your will.*
—*When you want to leave something to an organization or institution that was not mentioned in your will.*
—*When the condition of your health changes.*
—*When you sell your personal residence.*
—*When someone mentioned in your will predeceases you.*

DEAR RICHARD E: Changing your will is not too much more difficult than changing your socks. If you have not changed your will in twenty years, it is certainly time you took another look at it. Surely in that time, the condition of your assets has changed. You may have quite a bit in your pension fund or built up your stock portfolio. Do take another look at your assets and at your will to decide if it is time for a new one.

You may change your will at any time. Simply destroy the old one and execute a new and valid one in its place.

You may simply want to make some minor changes in a will that you are otherwise satisfied with. This can be done by amending the will with a codicil. The codicil is simply added on to the old will, but it must be signed by you and witnessed again, just like the original will. It does not supersede or revoke the old will, but becomes a part of it.

Problems might be created with a codicil if it is inconsistent with any of the items or conditions in the will, or if it creates ambiguity in interpreting the intent of the will. In other words, it must not contradict any of the previous conditions set forth in the original will. It can be safely used, say in a situation where you simply want a newly purchased automobile to go to your daughter, instead of your spouse.

Sometimes it is safer to take the long route and execute a totally new will.

Your will is a document that you should review periodically, especially when any of the events listed in the left column take place.

10. What Are The Contents
   Of A Will?

DEAR MR. ANSWERMAN: I am in the process of preparing a new will, since I have just moved to another state and retired.

Do all wills have the same parts? What should I look for in terms of specific clauses and terms in a will? What if the form I buy in the store doesn't have a provision I need to add to my will?

Ginger T., Seattle, WA

BASIC PARTS OF A WILL:

--Your name (all the names you have ever used, including your maiden name)
--Your residence
--A statement revoking prior wills
--Funeral arrangements
--Debts
--Administrative expenses
--Gifts and bequests
--Residue clause
--Rights of surviving spouse
--Bequests to children and relatives
--Guardian for minor children
--Special provisions for adult disabled child
--Common disaster clause
--Tax provisions
--A personal representative

DEAR GINGER T: The basic provisions of wills are generally the same, but you can always add other provisions as they apply to your particular situation.

While your wishes about the disposal of your body at your death can be included in your will, it is a good idea to have it in a separate letter because your will might not be read immediately after your death.

A residue clause should be included to cover situations where one or more of your beneficiaries might predecease you and you have not changed your will. The bequest you make to a beneficiary who dies before you will go to that person's heirs unless you specify otherwise. Or you may leave your estate to your children, one of whom dies before you, but has children. You may want grandchildren to get their parent's portion of your estate. This information has to be stated in the residue clause.

Your surviving spouse retains rights even in cases where you may be legally separated, even when they waive certain rights before your death. There are legal minimums that spouses are entitled to. It is a good idea to refer to a spouse by name in a will, especially if you have been married more than once.

The word "issue" is used to refer to your descendants -- children and grandchildren. Special attention should be given to minor and disabled children when preparing your will. You will have to name a legal guardian for the child or disabled adult child to administer the inheritance.

A common disaster clause is included in the event both spouses die simultaneously.

APPENDIXES

I: MEDICARE CARRIERS BY STATE

ALABAMA
Medicare/Blue Cross Blue Shield
P.O. Box 830-140, Birmingham, AL 35282
1-800-292-8855 • 205-988-2244

ALASKA
Medicare/Aetna Life & Casualty
200 S.W. Market St., P.O. Box 1992
Portland, OR 97207-1998
1-800-547-6333

ARIZONA
Medicare/Aetna Life & Casualty
P.O. Box 37200, Phoenix, AZ 85069
1-800-352-0411 • 602-861-1968

ARKANSAS
Medicare/Ark. Blue Cross & Blue Shield
P.O. Box 1418, Little Rock, AR 72203
1-800-482-5525 • 501-378-2320

CALIFORNIA
*Counties of: Los Angeles, Orange,
San Diego, Ventura, Imperial, San Luis
Obispo, Santa Barbara*
Medicare/Transamerica Occidental Life
Insurance Co.
Box 50061, Upland, CA 91785-0061
1-800-252-9020 • 213-748-2311

Rest of State: Medicare Claims Dept.
Blue Shield of California
Chico, CA 95976
(In area codes 209, 408, 415, 707, 916)
1-800-952-8627
(In area codes 213, 619, 714, 805, 818)
1-800-848-7713 • 714-824-0900

COLORADO
Medicare/Blue Shield of Colorado
P.O. Box 173520, Denver, CO 80217
1-800-332-6681 • 303-831-2661

CONNECTICUT
Medicare/The Travelers Ins. Co.
P.O. Box 5005, Wallingford, CT 06493-5005
1-800-982-6819
(In Hartford) 203-728-6783

DELAWARE
Medicare/Pennsylvania Blue Shield
P.O. 890200, Camp Hill, PA 17089-0200
1-800-851-3535

DISTRICT OF COLUMBIA
Medicare/Pennsylvania Blue Shield
P.O. 890200, Camp Hill, PA 17089-0200
1-800-233-1124

FLORIDA
Medicare/Blue Shield of Florida, Inc.
P.O. Box 2525, Jacksonville, FL 32231
1-800-333-7586 • 904-355-3680

GEORGIA
The Prudential Ins. Co. of America
Medicare Part B
P.O. Box 546, Buford, GA 30518
1-800-727-0827

HAWAII
Medicare/Aetna Life & Casualty
P.O. Box 3947
Honolulu, HI 96812
1-800-242-5242 • 808-524-1240

IDAHO
Medicare/Equicor-Equitable HCA Corp.
P.O. Box 8048, Boise, ID 83707
1-800-627-2782 • 208-342-7763

ILLINOIS
Medicare Claims
Blue Cross & Blue Shield of Illinois
P.O. Box 4422, Marion, IL 62959
1-800-642-6930 • 312-938-8000

INDIANA
Medicare Part B
Associated Ins. Companies, Inc.
P.O. Box 7073, Indianapolis, IN 46207
1-800-622-4792 • 317-842-4151

IOWA
Medicare/Blue Shield of Iowa
636 Grand, Des Moines, IA 50309
1-800-532-1285 • 515-245-4785

KANSAS
Counties of: Johnson, Wyandotte
Medicare/Blue Shield of Kansas City
P.O. Box 419840, Kansas City, MO 64141
1-800-892-5900 • 816-561-0900

Rest of State:
Medicare/Blue Shield of Kansas
P.O. Box 239, Topeka, KS 66629
1-800-432-3531 • 913-232-3773

KENTUCKY
Medicare Part B
Blue Cross & Blue Shield of Kentucky
100 East Vine St., Lexington, KY 40507
1-800-999-7608 • 606-233-1441

LOUISIANA
Blue Cross & Blue Shield of Louisiana
P.O. Box 95024
Baton Rouge, LA 70895-9024
1-800-462-9666
(In New Orleans) 504-529-1494
(In Baton Rouge) 504-379-8400

MAINE
Medicare/Blue Shield of Mass/Tri-State
P.O. Box 1010, Biddeford, ME 04005
1-800-492-0919 • 207-282-5991

MARYLAND
Counties of: Montgomery, Prince George's
Medicare/Pennsylvania Blue Shield
P.O. 890100, Camp Hill, PA 17089-0100
1-800-233-1124 • 717-763-3601

Rest of State: Maryland Blue Shield, Inc.
1946 Greenspring Dr.
Timonium, MD 21093
1-800-492-4795 • 301-561-4160

MASSACHUSETTS
Medicare/Blue Shield of Mass., Inc.
P.O. Box 1000, Rockland, MA 02371
1-800-882-1228 • 617-956-3994

MICHIGAN
Medicare Part B
Michigan Blue Cross & Blue Shield
P.O. Box 2201, Detroit, MI 48231-2201
(In area code 313) 1-800-482-4045
(In area code 517) 1-800-322-0607
(In area code 616) 1-800-442-8020
(In area code 906) 1-800-562-7802
(In Detroit) 313-225-8200

MINNESOTA
*Counties of: Anoka, Dakota, Filmore,
Goodhue, Hennepin, Houston, Olmstead,
Ramsey, Wabasha, Washington, Winona*
Medicare/The Travelers Ins. Co.
8120 Penn Avenue
South Bloomington, MN 55431
1-800-352-2762 • 1-800-382-2000
612-884-7171

Rest of State:
Medicare/Blue Shield of Minnesota
P.O. Box 64357, St. Paul, MN 55164
1-800-392-0343 • 612-456-5070

MISSISSIPPI
Medicare/The Travelers Ins. Co.
P.O. Box 22545, Jackson, MS 39225-2545
1-800-682-5417 • 601-977-5500

MISSOURI
*Counties of Andrew, Atchison, Bates,
Benton, Buchanan, Caldwell, Carroll,
Cass, Clay, Clinton, Daviess, DeKalb,
Gentry, Grundy, Harrison, Henry, Holt,
Jackson, Johnson, Lafayette, Livingston,
Mercer, Nodaway, Pettis, Platte, Ray, St.
Clair, Saline, Vernon, Worth*
Medicare/Blue Shield of Kansas City
P.O. Box 419840, Kansas City, MO 64141
1-800-892-5900 • 816-561-0900

Rest of State: Medicare
General American Life Insurance Co.
P.O. Box 505, St. Louis, MO 63166
1-800-392-3070 • 314-843-8880

MONTANA
Medicare/Blue Shield of Montana, Inc.
P.O. Box 4310, Helena, MT 59604
1-800-332-6146 • 406-444-8350

NEBRASKA
Medicare
P.O. Box 239, Topeka, KS 66629
913-232-3773

NEVADA
Medicare/Aetna Life & Casualty
P.O. Box 37230, Phoenix, AZ 85069
1-800-528-0311

NEW HAMPSHIRE
Medicare
Blue Shield of Massachusetts/Tri-State
P.O. Box 1010, Biddeford, ME 04005
1-800-447-1142 • 207-282-5689

NEW JERSEY
Medicare
The Prudential Insurance Co. of America
P.O. Box 400010, Harrisburg, PA 17140
1-800-462-9306

NEW MEXICO
Medicare/Aetna Life & Casualty
P.O. Box 25500
Oklahoma City, OK 73125-0500
1-800-423-2925
(in Albuquerque) 505-843-7771

NEW YORK
Counties of: Bronx, Columbia, Delaware,
Dutchess, Greene, Kings, Nassau, New York,
Orange, Putnam, Richmond, Rockland,
Suffolk, Sullivan, Ulster, Westchester
Medicare/Empire Blue Cross & Blue Shield
P.O. Box 4840, Grand Central Station
New York, NY 10163
1-800-442-8430 • 212-490-4444

County of Queens
Medicare/Group Health, Inc.
P.O. Box A966, Times Square Station
New York, NY 10036
212-760-6790

Rest of State: Medicare
Blue Shield of Western New York
P.O. Box 600, Binghamton, NY 13902-5200
1-800-252-6550 • 607-772-9606

NORTH CAROLINA
The Prudential Insurance Co. of America
Medicare B Division
P.O. Box 2126, High Point, NC 27261
1-800-672-3071

NORTH DAKOTA
Medicare/Blue Shield of North Dakota
4510 13th Avenue, S.W.
Fargo, ND 58121-0001
1-800-437-4762 • 701-282-0691

OHIO
Medicare/Nationwide Mutual Ins. Co.
P.O. Box 57, Columbus, OH 43216
1-800-282-0530 • 614-249-7157

OKLAHOMA
Medicare/Aetna Life & Casualty
701 N.W. 63rd St., Suite 300
Oklahoma City, OK 73116-7693
1-800-522-9079 • 405-848-7711

OREGON
Medicare/Aetna Life & Casualty
200 S.W. Market St., P.O. Box 1997
Portland, OR 97207-1997
1-800-452-0125 • 503-222-6831

PENNSYLVANIA
Medicare/Pennsylvania Blue Shield
Box 890065, Camp Hill, PA 17089-0065
1-800-382-1274

RHODE ISLAND
Medicare/Blue Shield of Rhode Island
1 Weybosset Hill, Providence, RI 02901
1-800-662-5170 • 401-861-2273

SOUTH CAROLINA
Medicare Part B
Blue Cross & Blue Shield of
South Carolina
Fontaine Road Business Center
300 Arbor Lake Drive, Suite 1300
Columbia, SC 29223
1-800-868-2522 • 803-754-0639

SOUTH DAKOTA
Medicare Part B
Blue Shield of North Dakota
4510 13th Avenue, S.W.
Fargo, ND 58121-0001
1-800-437-4762

TENNESSEE
Medicare
The Equitable Life Assurance Society
P.O. Box 1465, Nashville, TN 37202
1-800-342-8900 • 615-244-5650

TEXAS
Medicare
Blue Cross & Blue Shield of Texas, Inc.
P.O. Box 660031, Dallas, TX 75266-0031
1-800-442-2620 • 214-669-6900

UTAH
Medicare/Blue Shield of Utah
P.O. Box 30269
Salt Lake City, UT 84130-0270
1-800-426-3477 • 801-481-6196

VERMONT
Medicare
Blue Shield of Massachusetts/Tri-State
P.O. Box 1010, Biddeford, ME 04005
1-800-447-1142 • 207-282-5991

VIRGINIA
Counties of Arlington, Fairfax;
Cities of: Alexandria, Falls Church, Fairfax
Medicare/Pennsylvania Blue Shield
Box 890109, Camp Hill, PA 17089-0109
1-800-233-1124

Rest of State: Medicare
The Travelers Ins. Co.
P.O. Box 26463
Richmond, VA 23260-6463
1-800-552-3423 • 804-330-4600

WASHINGTON
Mail to your local Medical Service Bureau.
If you do not know which bureau handles your
claim, mail to:

Medicare Washington Physicians' Service
4th and Battery Bldg., 6th floor
2401 4th Avenue, Seattle, WA 98121
(In King County) 1-800-422-4087
                  206-464-3711
(In Spokane)   1-800-572-5256
                  509-536-4550
(In Kitsap)   1-800-552-7114
                  206-377-5576
(In Pierce)   206-597-6530

WEST VIRGINIA
Medicare/Nationwide Mutual Ins. Co.
P.O. Box 57, Columbus, OH 43216
1-800-848-0106

WISCONSIN
Medicare/WPS
Box 1787, Madison, WI 53701
1-800-362-7221
(In Madison)   608-221-3330
(In Milwaukee)   414-931-1071

WYOMING
Medicare/Equitable Life Assurance Society
P.O. Box 628, Cheyenne, WY 82003
1-800-442-2371 • 307-632-9381

AMERICAN SAMOA
Medicare/Aetna Life & Casualty
P.O. Box 3947, Honolulu, HI 96812
808-524-1240

GUAM
Medicare/Aetna Life & Casualty
P.O. Box 3947, Honolulu, HI 96812
808-524-1240

PUERTO RICO
Medicare/Seguros De Servicio De
Salud De Puerto Rico
Call Box MCA, Hato Rey, PR 00936
1-800-462-7385 • 809-749-4949

VIRGIN ISLANDS
Medicare/Seguros De Servicio De
Salud De Puerto Rico
Call Box MCA, Hato Rey, PR 00936
1-800-462-7385 • 809-749-4949

Monthly Benefits at Age 65

YOUR AGE IN 1991	WHO RECEIVES BENEFITS	YOUR PRESENT ANNUAL EARNINGS				
		$12,000	$20,000	$30,000	$42,000	$53,400 AND UP
65	You	$502	$695	$916	$983	$1,022
	Spouse or child	251	347	458	491	511
64	You	512	709	936	1,006	1,049
	Spouse or child	256	354	468	503	524
63	You	513	710	937	1,010	1,056
	Spouse or child	256	355	468	505	528
62	You	505	700	923	997	1,045
	Spouse or child	252	350	461	498	522
61	You	506	701	928	1,004	1,1,055
	Spouse or child	253	350	464	502	527
55	You	512	710	939	1,041	1,117
	Spouse or child	256	355	469	520	558
50	You	493*	686*	905*	1,023*	1,115*
	Spouse or child	258	359	473	535	583
45	You	486*	677*	889*	1,019*	1,128*
	Spouse or child	260	362	476	546	604
40	You	490*	684*	894*	1,030*	1,156*
	Spouse or child	262	366	479	552	619
35	You	495*	691*	899*	1,037*	1,169*
	Spouse or child	265	370	481	555	626
30	You	463*	648*	839*	969*	1,093*
	Spouse or child	267	373	484	559	630

* These amounts are reduced for retirement at age 65 because the Normal Retirement Age (NRA) is higher for these persons; the reduction factors are different for the worker and the spouse.

III: CHECKLIST OF ESSENTIAL DOCUMNETS

Check the items that apply to you, and then make sure you know where they are located.

_____ birth certificates for immediate family

_____ naturalization papers

_____ adoption papers

_____ marriage certificates

_____ divorce decrees

_____ social security cards

_____ social security earnings record

_____ pension benefit statements (private and government)

_____ military records (commissions, discharge, Veteran's)

_____ bank names, adresses, account numbers

_____ life insurance policies

_____ home and health/accident insurance policies

_____ itemized list of investments (certificates of deposit, stock certificates, bonds, U.S. savings bonds)

_____ federal, state and local income tax returns (3 years)

_____ other tax statements (such as property)

_____ real estate deeds, mortgages, titles, notes

_____ apartment and condominium leases

_____ automotive title, registration, bill of sale

_____ credit payments and status

_____ loans you owe and status

_____ loans owed you and status

_____ business and partnership agreements

_____ wills (yours and your spouses)

_____ trust agreements

_____ declared value of household goods and collectibles

IV: AGING INFORMATION STATE DIRECTORY

ALABAMA

Commission on Aging
State Capitol
Montgomery, Ala. 36130
(205) 261-5743

ALASKA

Older Alaskans Commission
Pouch C, Mail Stop 0209
Juneau, Alaska 99811
(907) 465-3250

ARIZONA

Aging and Adult Administration; (P.O. Box 6123)
1400 West Washington St.
Phoenix, Ariz. 85005
(602) 255-4446

ARKANSAS

Arkansas State Office on Aging
Donaghey Building, suite 1428, 7th & Main Sts.
Little Rock, Ark. 72201
(501) 371-2441

CALIFORNIA

Department of Aging
1020 19th St.
Sacramento, Calif. 95814
(916) 322-5290

COLORADO

Aging and Adult Services Division
Department of Social Services, room 503, 1575 Sherman St.
Denver, Colo. 80220
(303) 866-2586

CONNECTICUT

Department on Aging
175 Main Street
Hartford, Conn. 06106
(203) 566-7725

DELAWARE

Division of Aging
Department of Health and Social Services
1901 North Dupont Highway
New Castle, Del. 19720
(302) 421-6791

DISTRICT OF COLUMBIA

Executive Director, Office on Aging, Office of the Mayor
1424 K St., NW.
Washington, D.C. 20005
(202) 724-5622

FLORIDA

Program Office of Aging and Adult Services
Department of Health and Rehabilitation Services
1323 Winewood Blvd.
Tallahassee, Fla. 32301
(904) 488-8922

GEORGIA

Office of Aging
878 Peachtree Street, N.E., Room 632
Atlanta, Ga. 30309
(404) 894-5333

HAWAII

Executive Office on Aging, Office of the Governor, State of Hawaii
1149 Bethel Street, room 307
Honolulu, Hawaii 96813
(808) 548-2593

IDAHO

Idaho Office on Aging
Room 114-Statehouse
Boise, Idaho 83720
(208) 334-3833

ILLINOIS

Department on Aging
421 East Capitol Ave.
Springfield, Ill. 62706
(217) 785-3356

INDIANA

Indiana Department on Aging & Community Services
Suite 1350, 115 N. Pa. St.
Indianapolis, Ind. 46204
(317) 232-7006

IOWA

Commission on Aging
914 Grand Avenue, Suite 236, Jewett Bldg.
Des Moines, Iowa 50319
(515) 281-5187

KANSAS

Department of Aging
610 West 10th St.
Topeka, Kans. 66612
(913) 296-4986

KENTUCKY

Division for Aging Services, Department of Human Resources
DHR Bldg., 6th floor, 275 East Main St.
Frankfort, Ky. 40601
(502) 564-6930

LOUISIANA

Office of Elderly Affairs
4528 Bennington Ave., P.O. Box 80374
Baton Rouge, La. 70898-0374
(504) 925-1700

MAINE

Bureau of Maine's Elderly, Department of Human Services
State House, Station No. 11
Augusta, Maine 04333
(207) 289-2561

MARYLAND

Office on Aging, State Office Bldg.
301 West Preston St.
Baltimore, Md. 21201
(301) 383-5064

MASSACHUSETTS

Secretary, Department of Elder Affairs
38 Chauncy St.
Boston, Mass. 02111
(617) 727-7751

MICHIGAN

Office of Services to the Aging
P.O. Box 30026
Lansing, Mich. 48909
(517) 373-8230

MINNESOTA

Minnesota Board on Aging
Metro Square Bldg., room 204
7th and Robert Sts.
St. Paul Minn. 55101
(612) 296-2544

MISSISSIPPI

Mississippi Council on Aging
Executive Building, suite 301
Jackson, Miss. 39201
(601) 354-6590

MISSOURI

Division on Aging, Department of Social Services
Broadway State, P.O. Box 570
Jefferson City, Mo. 65101
(314) 751-3082

MONTANA

Community Services Division
P.O. Box 4210
Helena, Mont. 59604
(406) 444-3865

NEBRASKA

Department on Aging
P.O. Box 95044, 301 Centennial Mall South
Lincoln, Nebr. 68509
(402) 471-2306

NEVADA

Division for Aging Services, Department of Human Resources
505 East King St., Kinkead Bldg., room 101
Carson City, Nev. 89710
(702) 885-4210

NEW HAMPSHIRE

Council on Aging
14 Depot St.
Concord, N.H. 03301
(603) 271-2751

NEW JERSEY

Division on Aging
Department of Community Affairs
363 West State St., CN 807
Trenton N.J. 08625-0807
(609) 292-4833

OHIO

Ohio Department of Aging
50 West Broad St., 9th Floor
Columbus, Ohio 43215
(614) 466-5500

OKLAHOMA

Special Unit on Aging, Department of Human Services
P.O. Box 25352
Oklahoma City, Okla. 73125
(405) 521-2281

OREGON

Oregon Senior Services Division
313 Public Service Bldg.
Salem, Oreg. 97310
(503) 378-4728

PENNSYLVANIA

Department of Aging
231 State St., Room 307, Finance Bldg.
Harrisburg, Pa. 17120
(717) 783-1550

RHODE ISLAND

Department of Elderly Affairs
79 Washington St.
Providence, R.I. 02903
(401) 277-2858

SOUTH CAROLINA

Commission on Aging
915 Main St.
Columbia, S.C. 29201
(803) 758-2576

SOUTH DAKOTA

Office of Adult Services and Aging, Department of Social Services
Richard F. Kneip Bldg., 700 North Illinois St.
Pierre, S. Dak. 57501-2291
(605) 773-3656

NEW MEXICO

State Agency on Aging
224 East Palace Ave., 4th floor
La Villa Rivera Building
Santa Fe, N. Mex. 87501
(505) 827-7640

NEW YORK

Office for the Aging, New York State Executive Department
Empire State Plaza, Agency Building No. 2
Albany, N.Y. 12223
(518) 474-5731

NORTH CAROLINA

Division of Aging
708 Hillsboro St., suite 200
Raleigh, N.C. 27603
(919) 733-3983

NORTH DAKOTA

Aging Services, Department of Human Services
State Capitol Bldg.
Bismarck, N. Dak. 58505
(701) 224-2577

TENNESSEE

Commission on Aging
703 Tennessee Bldg., 535 Church St.
Nashville, Tenn. 37219
(615) 741-2056

TEXAS

Texas Department on Aging
210 Barton Springs Rd., 5th floor, P.O. Box 12786, Capital Station
Austin, Tex. 78704
(512) 475-2717

UTAH

Division of Aging and Adult Services, Department of Social Services
150 West North Temple, Box 2500
Salt Lake City, Utah 84110-2500
(801) 533-6422

VERMONT

Office on Aging
103 South Main St.
Waterbury, Vt. 05676
(802) 241-2400

VIRGINIA

Office on Aging
101 N. 14th St., 18th floor, James Monroe Bldg.
Richmond, Va. 23219
(804) 225-2271

WASHINGTON

Bureau of Aging and Adult Services
Department of Social and Health Services, OB-43G
Olympia, Wash. 98504
(206) 753-2502

WEST VIRGINIA

Commission on Aging
State Capitol
Charleston, W. Va. 25305
(304) 348-3317

WISCONSIN

Bureau on Aging
1 West Wilson St., room 685
Madison, Wis. 53702
(608) 272-8606

WYOMING

State of Wyoming, Wyoming Commission on Aging
Hathaway Bldg., #139
Cheyenne, Wyo. 82002
(307) 777-7986

AMERICAN SAMOA

Territorial Aging Program, Government of American Samoa
Office of the Governor
Pago Pago, American Samoa 96799
Samoa 3-1254 or 3-4116

GUAM

Office of Aging, Social Service
Department of Public Health, Government of Guam
P.O. Box 2618
Agana, Guam 96910
749-9901 extension 423

PUERTO RICO

Gericulture Commission, Department of Social Services
P.O. Box 11398
Santurce, P.R. 00910
(809) 722-2429

TRUST TERRITORY OF THE PACIFIC ISLANDS

Office on Aging
Trust Territory of the Pacific Islands
Saipan, CM 96950
Telephone Nos. 9335 or 9328

VIRGIN ISLANDS

Commission on Aging
6F Havensight Mall
Charlotte Amalie
St. Thomas, Virgin Islands 00801
(809) 774-5884

V: SOCIAL SECURITY ADMINISTRATION (SSA)

REGIONAL OFFICE TELEPHONE CONTACTS

Regional Office	Contact Person	Telephone Number
Boston	Pamela Lawrence	617-565-2881 FTS 835-2881
New York	Marie Cox	212-264-4989 FTS 264-4989
	Ed Conta	212-264-4991 FTS 264-4991
	Susan Jacobs	212-264-4990 FTS 264-4990
Philadelphia	Ed Keegan	215-597-9250 FTS 597-9250 or 215-597-9980 FTS 597-9980
Atlanta	Cammie Bohanon	404-331-3197 FTS 841-3197
Chicago	Rich Rouse	312-353-3983 FTS 353-3983
Dallas	Mary Stewart	214-767-4191 FTS 729-4191
Kansas City	Ken Bischof	816-426-6191 FTS 867-6191
Denver	Mike Gradel	303-844-2471 FTS 564-2471
	Gini Werder	303-844-2472 FTS 564-2472
San Francisco	Eddie Cooksey	415-744-4499 FTS 484-4499
Seattle	George Perry	206-442-2713 FTS 399-2713
	Ella Marie Washatka	206-442-2713 FTS 399-2713

REGIONAL OFFICE ADDRESSES AND SERVICE AREAS

Regional Office	Mailing Address	Service Area
Boston	Office of the Regional Commissioner Social Security Administration Room 1100, JFK Federal Building Boston, Massachusetts 02203	Connecticut, Maine Massachusetts, New Hampshire, Rhode Island, Vermont
New York	Office of the Regional Commissioner Social Security Administration Room 40-102, 26 Federal Plaza New York, New York 10278	New Jersey, New York, Puerto Rico, Virgin Islands
Philadelphia	Office of the Regional Commissioner Social Security Administration P.O. Box 8788 Philadelphia, Pennsylvania 19101	Delaware, Maryland, Pennsylvania, Virginia, Washington, D.C., West Virginia
Atlanta	Office of the Regional Commissioner Social Security Administration Suite 1902 101 Marietta Tower Atlanta, Georgia 30323	Alabama, Florida, Georgia, Kentucky, Mississippi, North Carolina, South Carolina, Tennessee
Chicago	Office of the Regional Commissioner Social Security Administration 10th Floor, 105 West Adams Street Chicago, Illinois 60603	Illinois, Indiana, Michigan, Minnesota, Ohio, Wisconsin
Dallas	Office of the Regional Commissioner Social Security Administration Room 1440 1200 Main Tower Building Dallas, Texas 75202	Arkansas, Louisiana, New Mexico, Oklahoma, Texas
Kansas City	Office of the Regional Commissioner Social Security Administration Room 436, 601 East 12th Street Kansas City, Missouri 64106	Iowa, Kansas, Missouri, Nebraska
Denver	Office of the Regional Commissioner Social Security Administration Drawer 3618, 1961 Stout Street Denver, Colorado 80294	Colorado, Montana, North Dakota, South Dakota, Utah, Wyoming

REGIONAL OFFICE ADDRESSES AND SERVICE AREAS (continued)

Regional Office	Mailing Address	Service Area
San Francisco	Office of the Regional Commissioner Social Security Administration 7th Floor, 75 Hawthorne Street San Francisco, California 94105	Arizona, California, Hawaii, Nevada, Guam, American Samoa
Seattle	Office of the Regional Commissioner Social Security Administration Mail Stop RX 53, Blanchard Plaza 2201 6th Avenue Seattle, Washington 98121	Alaska, Idaho, Oregon, Washington

SSA Headquarters Address and Telephone Number

SSA is headquartered in Woodlawn, Maryland (just outside of Baltimore). SSA has regional offices in the ten Federal regional centers and has more than a thousand field offices located throughout the 50 States, in Washington, D.C., and in the U.S. territories. You may contact any one of our offices for assistance on a Social Security-related issue; we have provided addresses and telephone numbers for your use throughout this guide. If you would prefer to deal with our headquarters office, you may write to the Commissioner or our Office of Public Inquiries. On request, we will be glad to provide written replies to your telephone inquiries.

Letters to the Commissioner should be addressed:
>   The Honorable Gwendolyn S. King
>   Commissioner of Social Security
>   Baltimore, MD 21235

The telephone number of the Office of Public Inquiries is:
>   301*-965-7700 or FTS 625-7700

---

* **Area code changes to 410 in November 1991.**

VI: U.S. LABOR DEPARTMENT, LABOR-MANAGEMENT SERVICES ADMINISTRATION

UNITED STATES DEPARTMENT OF LABOR
LABOR-MANAGEMENT
  SERVICES ADMINISTRATION
ROOM N-5471
WASHINGTON, D.C. 20216

AREA OFFICES: Consult your local telephone directory listings under United States Government (blue pages) for the address and telephone numbe of the Labor-Management Services Administration office nearest you. Area offices are located in the following cities:

Atlanta, GA
Boston, MA
Buffalo, NY
Chicago, IL
Cleveland, OH
Covington, KY
Dallas, TX
Denver, CO
Detroit, MI
East Orange, NJ
Hato Rey, PR
Honolulu, HI
Kansas City, MO
Los Angeles, CA
Miami, FL
Minneapolis, MN
Nashville, TN
New Orleans, LA
New York, NY
Philadelphia, PA
Pittsuburgh, PA
San Francisco, CA
Seattle, WA
St. Louis, MO
Washington, DC

American Association of Retired Persons (AARP)
1909 K St., N.W.
Washington, D.C. 20049
(202) 872-4700

American Society of Aging
833 Market St., Suite 516
San Francisco, CA 94103
(415) 543-2617

The Gerontological Society
1411 K St., N.W., Suite 300
Washington, D.C. 20005
(202) 393-1411

Gray Panthers
311 S. Juniper St., Suite 601
Philadelphia, PA 19107
(215) 545-6555

National Association of Area Agencies on Aging
600 Maryland Ave., S.W.
West Wing, Suite 208
Washington, D.C. 20024
(202) 484-7520

National Association of Retired Federal Employees
1533 New Hampshire Avenue, N.W.
Washington, D.C. 20036
(202) 234-0832

National Association of State Units on Aging
600 Maryland Avenue, S.W., Suite 208
Washington, D.C. 20024
(202) 484-7182

National Caucus and Center on Black Aged
1424 K St., N.W.
Suite 500
Washington, D.C. 20005
(202) 637-8400

National Center on Rural Aging (NCRA)
c/o National Council on the Aging
600 Maryland Ave., S.W., West Wing 100
Washington, D.C. 20024
(202) 479-1200

National Citizens Coalition on Nursing Home Reform
1424 16th St., N.W., Suite L2
Washington, D.C. 20036
(202) 797-0657

National Council of Senior Citizens
925 15th St., N.W.
Washington, D.C. 20005
(202) 347-8800

National Council on the Aging
600 Maryland Avenue, S.W.
West Wing, Suite 100
Washington, D.C. 20024
(202) 479-1200

National Indian Council on Aging
P.O. Box 2088
Albuquerque, NM 87103
(505) 242-9505

National Pacific/Asian Resource Center on Aging
2033 6th Ave., Suite 410
Seattle, WA 98121
(206) 448-0313

Older Women's League
1325 G. St., N.W., Lower Level B
Washington, D.C. 20005
(202) 783-6686

Pension Rights Center
918 16th St., N.W., Suite 704
Washington, D.C. 20006
9202) 296-3776

Society for the Right to Die
250 W. 57 St.
New York, NY 10107
(212) 246-6973

Villers Foundation
1334 G St., N.W.
Washington, D.C. 20005
(202) 628-3030

VIII: LIST OF CHARTS, TABLES, LISTS, AND FORMS

Approximate Monthly Benefits At Full Retirement Age And Steady Lifetime Earnings	5
Request For Earnings and Benefit Estimate	6
Age to Receive Full SS Benefits	8
Increases For Delayed Retirement	8
Percent Of Aged Receiving Pensions	10
SS And Equivalent Railroad Retirement Benefits Worksheet	13
Conditions Under Which Modified Formula Does Not Apply	20
Phase-In Factors For Reduced Benefits	20
Schedule Of Factor Reduction Percentages	21
Earnings For Credit Years Schedule	21
Evidence To Be Submitted By Claimant - Documents Chart	29
Marriage/Divorce Form	30
Benefit For Recomputation Form	31
Verification Of Benefits Form	32
Start/Stop Work Notice Form	33
Change Of Address Form	34
Report Of Death Form	35
Chart For Figuring Reduced Benefits	39
List of VA Offices	54
Savings Withdrawal Chart	62
Budget Today Worksheet	71
Projecting Retirement Income For Inflation	72
Retirement Budget Worksheet	73
Net Worth Worksheet	75
Average Annual Expenditures Chart - Older Households	76
Medicare (Part A) Covered Services	87
Medicare (Part B) Covered Services	88
Disability Benefits Chart	106
Net Worth Worksheet	122

IX: LIST OF QUESTIONS

WHAT YOUR GOVERNMENT OWES YOU

1. What Is Social Security?   3
2. How Much Will My Retirement Benefit Be?   4
3. What Is Full Retirement Age?   7
4. What Is Delayed Retirement?   9
5. Is SS Enough By Itself?   10
6. What If I Work After Retirement?   11
7. What Portion Of My SS Will Be Taxed?   12
8. How Do I Appeal A Decision On My SS Benefit?   14
9. Am I Allowed To Have A Representative Help Me?   15
10. How Much Can My Spouse And Children Get?   16

APPLYING FOR SOCIAL SECURITY

1. What Will I Need To Apply For SS?   17
2. How Can I Get Information About SS?   18
3. How Will My Pension Affect My SS Benefits?   19
4. What Is Acceptable Proof Of Marriage?   22
5. What Is Acceptable Proof Of Age?   23
6. How Do I Prove A Parent-Child Relationship?   24
7. How Will I Be Notified By SS?   25
8. Do I Have A Right To See My SS File?   26
9. Can A Creditor Attach My SS Benefits?   27
10. Can My SS Benefits Be Terminated?   28

KNOWING MORE ABOUT SSI

1. What Is SSI?   36
2. Who Qualifies For SSI?   37
3. How Much Can I Get From SSI?   38
4. How Can I Get Other Help?   40
5. How Much Income Can I Have And Still Collect SSI?   41
6. How Much Can I Own And Still Get SSI?   42
7. What Are The Residency Requirements For SSI?   43
8. How Do I Sign Up For SSI?   44
9. Can I Work Part-Time And Collect SSI?   45
10. What Is The SSI Appeal Process?   46

WHAT YOU SHOULD KNOW ABOUT PRIVATE PENSIONS

1. What Do I Need To Know About My Company's
   Pension Plan?   47
2. What Is Vesting?   48
3. What Is ERISA?   49
4. Should I Receive A Lump Sum Or Monthly Payments? 50
5. Are Survivors Protected Under Private Pension Plans? 51
6. What Are The Benefits For Federal Employees?   52
7. Who Is Entitled To Railroad Retirement Benefits? 53
8. Are There Any Retirement Benefits In Life Insurance? 58
9. What Are The Advantages Of Buying An Annuity?   59
10. What Are Some Good Investing Strategies?   60

IRAs AND OTHER INVESTMENTS

1. How Much Should I Set Aside In Savings?   61
2. What Are Some Other Risk-Free Alternatives?   63
3. What Are The Advantages Of IRAs and Keoghs?   64
4. How Good Are Bonds For Retirement?   65
5. Should I Invest In The Stock Market?   66
6. Where Should I Live In Retirement?   67
7. Is Real Estate Still A Good Investment?   68
8. What Are Some Home Equity Conversion Plans?   69
9. How Do I Prepare A Retirement Budget?   70
10. How Do I Estimate My Net Worth?   74

MEDICARE, MEDICAID, AND NURSING HOMES

1. How Does Medicare Protect Income?   77
2. Do I Need Private Medical Insurance Besides
   Medicare?   78
3. What Is The Difference Between Medicare And
   Medicaid?   79
4. Does Medicare Cover Home Health Care?   80
5. How Do I Apply For Medicare?   81
6. Can I Find Out Why I Was Turned Down
   By Medicaid?   82
7. Who Decides Reasonable And Necessary Services?   83
8. What Is A Nursing Home?   84
9. How Expensive Are Nursing Homes?   85
10. Does A Nursing Home Resident Have Rights?   86

KNOWING MORE ABOUT EARNED INCOME

1. What Is Self-Employment Income?   89
2. How Do I Report Tips?   90
3. What Tax Return Forms Do Employers Use?   91
4. How Can I Get Help On Self-Employment
      Tax Payments?   92
5. Should I Or Shouldn't I Retire?   93
6. How Many People Over 65 Still Work?   94
7. Can I Get Tax Counseling?   95
8. Can I Afford To Stop Working After Retirement?   96
9. How Does Social Security Know About My Earnings?   97
10. What If Social Security Says I Was Overpaid?   98

TAX CREDITS AND DISABILITY

1. Who Must File A Return?   99
2. What Are Exemptions?   100
3. What Are Special Tax Breaks?   101
4. Should I Itemize Deductions?   102
5. Are There Special Credits For The Elderly and
      Disabled?   103
6. Is There Credit For Dependent Care?   104
7. What Are The Disability Benefits For Older Persons?   105
8. How Is Disability Determined?   107
9. What Are The "Listings"?   108
10. What Are The "Grids"?   109

FIGHTING AGE DISCRIMINATION IN EMPLOYMENT

1. Is Age Discrimination In Employment Illegal?   110
2. Who Is Protected By The ADEA?   111
3. How Can Discrimination Be Proven?   112
4. Are There Other Standards For Age Discrimination?   113
5. Are There State Laws Prohibiting Age Discrimination?   114
6. How Can I File An Age Discrimination Complaint?   115
7. What EEOC Procedures Enforce ADEA?   116
8. When Do I Take A Private Lawsuit?   117
9. Is There Protection Against Discrimination From
      Goverment Services?   118
10. If I Win A Case, Will I Receive Back Pay?   119

1. What Is The Importance Of Estate Planning?   120
2. How Do I Make An Inventory Of My Property?   121
3. What Is The Tax Liability Of My Estate?   123
4. What Deductions Can I Use On My Federal Estate Tax?   124
5. What Is The Gift Tax?   125
6. What Are Gifts To A Spouse?   126
7. What Is The Language Of Wills?   127
8. Can A Will Be Changed?   128
9. How Do I Create A Will?   129
10. What Goes Into The Contents Of A Will?   130

NOTES